PROPERTY NOMAD

How to Create a Property Business
You Can Run from Anywhere

Benn,
All the best
Peter Armistead.

Peter Armistead

Editing and formatting by Oxford Literary Consultancy.

www.oxfordwriters.com

Dedication

To my amazing wife, partner and the most gifted interior designer, Deborah Armistead. To my two children, Gabriel and Sadie, and to my mother and father who have been in the business since the very start.

To all the amazing people at Armistead Property I have the pleasure of working with, including: Sean Dunn, Simon James, Szczepan, Michal and Mateusz Mroczkowski, Julita Mrockowski, Franik, Dawid, Pawel, Dariusz, Pawel and Arek.

To all the professionals, investors and developers I work with daily including: John Appelby, Paul Cambell, Yvette Davis, Harry, Dave, Ellie, Maura and Oxanna at Jordan Fishwicks, Simon and Nicola at Emma Hattons, Mike Boggett, Yvette Davis, Sheldon Gaudet, Hannah Garcia, Tim Greenwood.

To the people who have had an amazing influence on my personal and athletic life including: Gary Robbins, Eric Carter, Chris Goodwin, Kevin Hodder, Keith Reid, Andy Mouncey.

Table of Contents

Foreword

In 2001, I left a very promising career as a City lawyer. I was earning good money and I was doing well and enjoying it. It was however still the life of an employee and I wanted more. I wanted to escape the nine-to-five rat race. I wanted a lifestyle of freedom. I wanted financial freedom and the freedom to choose how I spend my time. I did not want a boss dictating these things to me.

Today, I own an award-winning property business and have bought and sold nearly 500 properties. I am financially free and my working day is usually over by 10:00 a.m., leaving me the majority of the day to do what I choose. Best of all, I have done all of this whilst travelling the world, having some amazing experiences and working remotely. I spend 80 per cent of my time outside of the UK, yet my property business is solely focused in South Manchester within just a couple of post codes. Real estate investment has given me the ability to live my dreams. This is my story and is a blueprint of how you too can remotely set up and run a very successful multi-million pound real estate business. You can have the freedom to work from wherever you want, whatever hours you choose and do whatever you want with the majority of your day. You can have the lifestyle you desire.

SECTION 1

THE ADVENTURE BEGINS

Heart Rush

I'd never experienced such heart rush as I did the very first time I put a pair of skis on my feet.

I was absolutely exhilarated both by the sensation of movement and speed. I'm not alone — people everywhere find this sensation addictive whether they're surfing, mountain biking or skiing. They're fanatical about it. Once you've experienced it, you feel like you're only living half a life if you're not doing it. Always, the question at the back of your mind is: "How do I get this sensation of motion again, this feeling of being alive?" Now, I did play ball sports when I was a kid, and it was nice being outdoors feeling the sunshine and smelling the fresh-cut grass, but traditional ball sports just never blew me away. What does blow me away is being in the mountains, really being out there in nature and feeling responsible for managing yourself in the real outdoors. To me, that's "being outdoors" — not running around a man-made soccer pitch in a field in the middle of London.

That excitement of skiing paired with the tremendous beauty of the mountains is the real world for me.

I took my first ski trip around age twenty and after, became an obsessive skier. I primarily went to the French Alps — usually to Les Deux Alpes. In my twenties, I was a lawyer working in London and I didn't have a huge amount of leisure time. I would work in the office in London, Monday to Friday, and then at three o'clock on Friday would leave work, bang down to the airport, get on a plane, do a couple of days of skiing, and fly back that Sunday evening. I'd do that almost every weekend in the winter when I was a lawyer. I'd try to get as much skiing in as I possibly could – and I knew that I wanted to do a lot more skiing or even live in a ski resort. I knew my location would have to be the mountains, naturally, but which set of mountains? I researched and selected the best five ski resorts in the world for both skiing and general livability. I thought, "Well, I'll go to all five of these places and pick the one that suits me best. Then within the next year or two, I'll try to set up a life in the best one."

Whistler, Canada

The first time I travelled to Whistler, Canada, was in April 2001 for a one-week holiday with one of my good friends, Matt. We flew into Vancouver. Little did I know that this trip would change my life.

The journey up from the airport to Vancouver was probably the most spectacular journey that I'd ever been on — even though I've done loads of travelling. It's a world-famous road. They film lots of car adverts there, though I didn't know this at the time. I was surrounded by a big glacier range. The mountains are impressively high: sharp, alpine-like mountains that seem rooted in the spectacular turquoise of the ocean, which almost serves as a mirror for them. It truly is absolutely spectacular. In the ocean itself there's a whole bunch of islands all covered in big, old, evergreen trees that we don't have many of in England. On the other side, you're in a rainforest. I was fascinated: it felt so remote, like I was in a wilderness paradise far away from anything resembling a town or people, just thousands of miles of pure wilderness.

Of course, we eventually arrived at our destination: a small hotel in the village. Whistler is very efficient, very well run, with lots of emphasis on customer service and I was impressed by the actual ski resort itself and by what was going on in the village. Some good investment had been put into the resort in a way that I wasn't necessarily used to in the European ski resorts, where the customer service is much more haphazard. In contrast, Whistler was run by one big company so they could make better strategic decisions. I actually went during a bad snow season and in my mind it was better than some of the very best seasons that I'd ever experienced in Europe. The skiing was absolutely world class. I was able to do so much more skiing than I would have normally done in a day, just because it was so efficiently managed.

I spent a lot of time skiing through the trees, which was a fresh experience for me. You don't often ski through trees in Europe, whereas over in Whistler, it's lower down with less alpine and a lot more snow. Skiing through the trees was fantastic. You get the smell of the pine needles and woods and you really feel part of nature. The amount of snow over in Whistler in what they called a "bad" snow season was just ridiculous!

I've always been a morning person, so I loved to get up really early in the morning, go get a cup of coffee, and walk about the village. Now, if I were doing that in France you wouldn't see many people about — there'd probably just be little puddles of vomit in places from drunks staggering home the night before. In contrast, everything was immaculate at Whistler. It looked like a manicured bowling lawn. The resort had dozens of staff who were there cleaning up and gardening. They do so much more maintenance and looking after things than the English or Europeans do. I would see teams of good-looking, healthy girls going about in big vans picking up litter, gardening, and making the place look immaculate. I thought, "Wow. They've invested a lot of resources over here to be able to do that." In Europe, they tend to stick to the bare bones to make things happen, whereas at Whistler there were lots of nice extras to make the experience that much more impressive.

During that holiday, we didn't go on any day trips; we did all of our exploring on skis. We were on the first lift up and we would ski right until the end of the day. We skied as much as we possibly could. Some friends of ours who were living in Vancouver came and took us back country skiing away from the lifts, and we had to hike up mountains and ski down, which was fantastic.

I was enamored by British Columbia, and by Whistler in particular. By the time I was on the return flight back to London, I'd already decided that this was the place for me. I told Matt that Whistler was the lifestyle I wanted and I was going to resign from my job when I got back. I can remember him looking at me with a smile on his face, half laughing. It was half "Seriously?" and half, "Right, okay. I know this has been in the pipeline for a while, so this is the place, is it? This is going to happen?"

Although I'd thought about this before, it wasn't something I had been preparing for. So I was a bit nervous. I'd studied and worked hard to become a lawyer and it wasn't an easy decision to give it up. But I still knew that when I got back to the UK I was going to go resign and pursue a different and better life than the one I was leading.

My law years

Now, before I get any further, I should state that I actually loved my job as a lawyer and had a really good time working at my firm. I was good at my job and worked with some really intelligent, high-achieving people. I loved going to work and enjoyed the meetings and the banter. During my legal career, I worked in two different firms but my main one was working at an investment management company as their in-house lawyer. It was a really nice office with a great environment: marble floors, a five-level atrium, people wearing nice suits, and an office close to Oxford Circus in London.

My working environment was nice, but it was relatively bare: the window looked out onto another brick wall, desks remained unadorned with personal trinkets or family photos. The offices themselves were situated in beautiful buildings, and internally most of the offices were open plan. Because of the sensitive nature of my work (I was usually involved when a partner was being accused of being negligent) I had my own separate office. In that office I had a secretary, Kate, who was a great individual. It was just a small office with lots of books and files, like something from the David Brent TV series, *The Office.*

I had been very happy when I first got that job offer. I remember going to those offices and getting a good feel for what life there would be like. There were some good, sexy cases worth billions of pounds, which I would get to work on. I was over the moon to have gotten that job, so much so that during the negotiation of the salary process, I'd actually said, "When do you want me to start?"

They'd said, "Well, Monday morning would be great."

And I replied, "How about Monday morning in three months' time?" They agreed.

And instantly, I packed my backpack, flew to Nepal, and went to the Himalayas. I got a chance to get a cool mountain trip in before I actually went to work! Even then, the clues were there for where my heart truly lay. I always had an urge to go travelling and find a bit of adventure, especially where mountains were involved.

My co-workers and I were all relatively happy. I can't paint a picture of it being anything remotely bad; I had some fantastic times there. However, as I looked out of my window and saw nothing but a brick wall, I was reminded that this was not the lifestyle for me: there was no freedom. I knew there was a better lifestyle out there.

I felt almost like a battery chicken; there were lots of other chickens about that I could chat to and have a laugh with and we were well cared for in our environment, but really the thing that I wanted to do was just get out of that cage and run about. It was that simple and wasn't a surprise to me that I was subconsciously looking for a different kind of lifestyle, especially when you consider that I was working around the clock.

I was even sleeping in the office some nights. I once did six months solid, working every single day, including Saturdays and Sundays. That was at least ten hours on a Sunday, and the Mondays and Tuesdays would be 18-hour days. This was during a big trial we were doing which went on for about six months.

At the end of that trial, I went straight up to see my mum in Manchester. It was the first time in half a year I'd seen her. When she opened the door and saw me, she actually cried. She said, "You look grey and ill." I looked as though I had some sort of kidney disease because I hadn't seen daylight for about half a year. I'd just been working away and I was also a little bit skinny and weedy. So, I guess that's one negative about being a city lawyer: the lifestyle was not a good, healthy one.

My boss at my firm was landed gentry and he was very old-school. Back then, he was probably around 55 to 60 years old. Just at the end of my career as a lawyer, we started introducing dress-down Fridays and he pitched up in one of the thickest, heaviest green tweed Saville Row suits you can imagine. Everyone else was trying to look as though they were on a golf course – chinos and polo shirts – and he pitched up looking both fantastic and hilarious. He was a barrister, and he was a very clever guy. He was great with clients and I got on really well with him even though we were both very different characters. We were both very hardworking; we got things done. It was a good relationship. He was very well-respected in the city and lots of people knew him. So, to be working for him was a privilege.

As the in-house lawyer at an investment management company, my primary role was to represent our company whenever a client complained about us or whenever an individual tried to sue us (or *did* sue us). For example, if we were the administrators of a company and were called in to manage a semi-bankrupt defunct company, we would place it into receivership and then start liquidating the company. That was a normal business event that we carried out. Every now and again, the old owners would sue us saying, "Hang on. You didn't have any right to put us into receivership. You've handled the receivership in a bad way. If you hadn't put us into receivership, this company would now be worth £1 billion. You sold it off for a £100 million, therefore we're suing you for £900 million."

Sometimes we would be managing someone's personal fund for them, which would be worth maybe £100,000, and then someone would perhaps then write a letter of complaint saying, "You've been holding £50,000 of my money in a low-interest bank account for four months. That's unacceptable! I could do that myself. You've been negligent. You should have been making me 5 or 6 per cent per annum, so how about you give me an extra £3,000?" I'd have to deal with that type of case as well and work out what we did about it: were we liable, and should we pay them?

All sorts of cases would hit my desk (although they were always financial ones) and I would determine first if we were liable, and then the actual liability. I'd have to do everything with it — a lot of work — just to work out what was going on, and then I would be in charge of that case, managing that litigation.

My firm also owned about 20 properties both commercial and residential around the UK, and it was my boss's job to look after them. Any rent reviews that were coming, any disputes, any legal issues — he dealt with all of those. One day, he said, "I don't enjoy looking after real estate. It takes up a lot of my time. I'd be very happy not to have to do this."

So, at that point I said, "Well, I'll do it for you." Not only did it get me in his good books, but I was also really interested in real estate by that point. The way I saw it, if it took me an extra ten hours a week to do the work, I knew that it would be worth it as it would be great training to gain a better knowledge of real estate. Therefore, I took on all the real estate files as well.

To be honest, a lot of that six years blends into one. It can be summarised relatively quickly: I was a small cog in some very big, multi-billion pound cases. It was all an experience of working really hard and doing a lot of partying as well. We were doing very long days and then on a Friday night hitting the pub straight away. There weren't any glory moments and I didn't bring in clients worth billions or anything like that. I just very much got my head down, got it done, and did it well. At the end of the day, being a lawyer isn't glamorous, it's an enjoyable, safe, steady, well-rewarded career. It's not a dynamic, fantastic, "you're going to be a rally car driver" type of lifestyle. It's just not that.

And of course, once I'd been skiing, I wanted so much more...

Handing in my notice

That first Monday morning I got back from my trip to Whistler, I woke up, had a shower, and got myself into work nice and early. I was always the first person in, followed by my boss.

I'd already sent him an e-mail saying, "Can I have a quick chat with you please?" So as soon as he arrived, he came in and said, "What do you want to talk about? How was your holiday?"

I said, "To be honest, it was actually too good. I think I'm going to resign and move over there."

There was a long pause, then, "Okay. Seriously?"

"Yeah, I am being serious about this. This is going to happen."

So he dangled a carrot, "You know you've got partnership waiting for you next year. It's going to happen. Do you want me to expedite that for you?"

"No that's not it."

"Is it a money thing?"

I answered truthfully, "It's not a money thing. It's a lifestyle thing. You know I'm really into the outdoors and skiing. If I could make the job with you guys work over there, then I would. But I don't think it can."

This was back in the day before remote working, so this was not an option. And it wouldn't have worked anyway.

So that was it. He said, "Okay well thanks for letting me know. Obviously, I'd like to keep you as long as possible."

I replied, "Now that I'm going I'd rather just get out of here. But if you want, I can work up until the ski season starts in mid-November. So I can stay for the next five to six months if you want me to."

He kept me to that – in a nice way. He wanted me to stay as long as I possibly could. So, I worked up until the 1st of November and then got over to Whistler in time for the lifts opening.

Sleepless nights

The decision to resign was an easy one to make in many ways and a difficult one in others. I had a goal of living in the mountains and doing more skiing, of travelling to many different countries and getting as many experiences as I could. I wanted a non-traditional lifestyle. So it was easy in that sense. What wasn't as simple was living with the consequences of my decision, because the reality was that I was just about to lose a very decent, steady salary. I was a young city lawyer with partnership on a plate and the financial rewards were quite attractive. I had worked very hard to become a lawyer and achieve what I had achieved already. Was I really just going to throw this away and start from scratch?

I could rationalise it; I believed that I was going on to bigger and better things. But even though I was very confident about the outdoor lifestyle, I was not as confident about my ability to make as much money as I would be doing as a lawyer.

I'd gotten a bit ahead of myself in that I was jumping ship before I had a better financial ship to sail. I had to get my head around the fact that there was going to be now at least a few years where I wouldn't have the same income I'd had as a lawyer. I needed to get my business sorted out and figure out how to work abroad, and many other things.

That was okay, I told myself — *I could plan.* This was all well and good during the day, but every single night, as soon as I went to bed, the demons I shelved away all day would enter my dreams—more like nightmares — all of my worries and fears came to the fore. I used to wake up from nightmares, panicking that I'd done the wrong thing. I didn't want to be poor. That wasn't part of the plan. I am very motivated by money and it's always been a part of who I am and a way of measuring success and achievement for me. I've always thought on a financial wavelength and that was one of the reasons I became a lawyer. The nightmares happened each night for the whole of the six months before I actually went to Whistler. I couldn't stop my subconscious.

Burning my bridges

I've got to admit I was a little bit sad when the time came to leave my job. We did the normal stuff and we all went off to the pub after work. We partied and we had a great time. But waking up the morning after almost felt strange. Something was missing. There was a sense of loss. It felt like I'd been robbed of my life as a lawyer and I'd done it myself. I didn't have a category I could fit myself into any more. For the first time I felt like I was alone and self sufficient. I was a proper nomad now.

I was by myself and I had the ability to shape my own destiny. I couldn't just go put my lawyer's suit on and call myself a lawyer any more. I was cut loose. I was different now. I remember thinking, 'All right. Fine. That's the end of one part my life and the start of a new one.' It was like drawing a line between the two separate parts of my life. It was a strange situation.

Many people had said to me, "You can always come back, can't you?" I remember one guy in particular making a flippant comment, "Well, everyone here likes you, Pete. You're doing a great job I'm sure you can always come back." The implication was, "You can come back… if it doesn't work out for you."

But that wasn't what I was aiming for, so I went straight back to my office and phoned up the Law Society and asked them to take me off the roll of solicitors. It was probably a bit more dramatic for me than it was for them. They were just very confused by the whole thing when I told them what I wanted to do. They just said, "No it doesn't work like that. You can't just take yourself off the roll of solicitors. You get struck off for fraud and misconduct, but no-one takes themselves off."

"No, I'd like to take myself off."

"Well, we can do it. But why would you want to do that?"

"It doesn't really matter why I want to do it. It's not for any bad reason. I've not committed fraud. I don't want to be a lawyer any more. I don't want that safety net there."

And they replied, slightly bemused, "Okay. Give us your details and we'll see to it that it happens."

It was a huge moment for me and I'm sure it was absolutely the most trivial moment for the woman taking down my details. Her reaction was, "It doesn't work like that. No. No. You don't need to do that." She obviously thought it was a very strange request.

It's the cliché about burning your bridges. You burn your bridges so that you're absolutely putting your back to the wall and giving yourself no choice or options in a situation. There is no going back. That's what I was doing, literally. I didn't want a fall-back position. I wanted it to absolutely 100% feel that there was only one way forward. Just like the NASA motto, "Failure is not an option."

I was not going back to being a lawyer. I didn't want to be an employee any more. I wanted a better life and I had to make it work.

SECTION 2

THE LIFESTYLE LEAP

Interior of our award-winning development at Carlton Terrace

Real estate: my plan for success

When I arrived in Whistler, I knew I was going to pursue a different lifestyle. As a lawyer, I could have nice weekends away skiing. But I did not want to be just a weekend warrior. I wanted to go 100% into trying to be one of the world's best skiers. I wanted to be a big mountain skier, to go all over the world and achieve as much as I could with the sport. My plan was 80 per cent focused on changing myself from being a desk-bound lawyer to becoming an outdoorsman. Though of course, I wanted to be able to pursue this lifestyle while being financially successful.

When it comes to a lifestyle of outdoor sporting pursuits, the reality is that many people don't earn much money in the industry. For example, some people will actively set out to become ski instructors in order to work outdoors all day, every day doing the sport they love, yet they know that they will only earn a minimum wage doing so. Add to that the fact that they can only earn a living in this manner for six months of the year, and they end up going to work in a bar for the rest of the year. Also, if you get an injury, or the weather is bad, you don't work or get paid. That was never the lifestyle I wanted. I wanted all the benefits of being able to spend as much time outdoors as I was able to and I wanted a better income stream than when I was a lawyer, so I needed to work out how that was going to happen.

My original plan included a mixture of real estate investment and owning online businesses because that would give me the ability to work wherever I wanted through a laptop and a mobile phone. Now, the very first business that I set up was whilst I was still practising law. It was an online casino. This was way before online gambling became mainstream. I think I was one of the very first people in the UK to actually have an online gambling license. So, I set that business up. It worked to an extent and it gave me an income stream in the early days. But it wasn't as successful as I wanted it to be, and very quickly the profits made from real estate eclipsed the idea of owning an online casino. I sold that business within the first couple of years of leaving the law and turned my attention 100 per cent to real estate.

Back then, it was a different world. In 2001, buy-to-let mortgages were only just coming out. People did not work remotely like they do now. For instance, these days, I know dozens of people who are able to complete most of their work online and manage everything from their homes in Whistler. But at the turn of the century, this wasn't as typical.

I was trying to bridge two different worlds: skiing/travelling and real estate. For both of those areas I had mentors, but they were very different areas and there was not one person that was actually doing both of those things in the way that I wanted. So, I had to just say, "Okay I am not a stereotypical person. I'm going to live the life that I want and that involves being half businessman, half outdoor enthusiast. I'm going to make that work properly and get the best of both worlds, not some sort of compromise situation."

With real estate, I did not really have a structured financial plan at that stage per se. It was very much a case of: it's an asset class that everyone knows works and everyone's made money out of. Everyone that's ever owned a home pretty much has made money. I just needed to work out how I was going to make more money than the average person out of real estate. I didn't know how to do it other than buying properties and sitting there and watching them go up in value, but I knew there had to be a far better way of doing it than just that.

So, I had a vision of where I wanted to be, but no clear goals. It was more a lifestyle that I wanted for myself. I had a vision of me with a laptop travelling the world, skiing, and doing exactly what I wanted to do – total freedom and having the finances to do it. I didn't have a detailed plan of exactly what I would need to earn per month or how it was going to pan out.

I've always been quite adventurous and entrepreneurial. I was willing to get into something, knowing where I wanted to end up, but not really knowing the path I needed to take to get there. I was making this huge lifestyle leap even though I didn't know exactly what the business plan was going to be each month, each year or each five years to enable me to get to the financial goal that I wanted. Now, I needed to back up my decision with something of substance to enable me to live my dream.

My first property purchases

I had a little experience with property before I left for Canada. It must have been about 1997 when I bought my first house to live in and then renovated it.

It was an old, artist's studio situated in an old school, so it was a really cool building. It was nice: a very open plan type of space. It had a balcony in the middle of it, with double height ceilings. I absolutely loved it. I remember being so excited about the place that the very day I bought it, I went and slept there on the floor without any mattress or pillow or anything. I was simply over the moon.

It was a one-bedroom with a big cupboard, but I converted it into a two-bedroom. I changed the kitchen, repainted the walls, lived in it with one of my friends Paul, (he rented the cupboard from me!) for a couple of years. This was on the Islington-Holloway border in London. I primarily just wanted a cool pad that was close to the City and close to Islington centre, so I could live a nice lifestyle while working in the City. It was a great location. It was next to the Tube and main bus routes into the City and was in an edgy, but already desirable, location.

The financing for that property was a straightforward residential mortgage based on my salary as a lawyer. Back then, buy-to-let mortgages didn't actually exist (they technically first appeared in 1996 but they were not mainstream at all until a few years later, and really took off in 2005), so I just bought with a standard mortgage in the usual way.

I bought that property for about £80,000 at the time. It was great: I could get to work within 40 minutes or so, which for London was good. We had a great time there, but it was a small.

Within about 18 months, the property had increased in value from £80,000 to £120,000. That was when I actually realised, "Hang on, that's nearly as much money as I earn in my job." When I saw how much the property had gone up, it changed from being a cool place to actually being a really good money maker. I thought to myself, "I need to focus on this a little bit more. Let's take the money out of that and do it again. That way, instead of having one place that's going up by £25,000 a year, I've got two places going up by £50,000 a year." It wasn't rocket science. So, while my first property purchase was an emotional one, one that I really wanted to live in and enjoy, that was pretty much the last property I purchased with that kind of mindset. After that, everything with property, from property number two onwards, was all about looking at the financial side of the real estate.

At this stage I didn't have funds saved up to enable me to buy property number two, but I realised I could afford another property by re-mortgaging. So I remortgaged, pulled the money out, bought another place with a residential mortgage — this time in Brixton — and took my friend, Paul, who was renting from me, with me to the new place. I rented the Islington property to a lovely couple who were in the flat upstairs at the time and they lived there for a good few years.

My second property wasn't a big place either, but it did have three bedrooms. My thinking was, "I could move out of my place in Islington, rent it, and more than cover the mortgage. Then I could move into the three-bedroom place in Brixton, live in one bedroom, and rent the other two bedrooms out. That way, both of those two bedrooms would pay more than the mortgage." So, I was actually being subsidised to live there; it wasn't even living rent-free. It was purely a financial move, and a good one.

I stayed in the place in Brixton for about 18 months or so. I updated the kitchen, repainted, pulled up the carpets and sanded down the wooden floors, so we ended up with a really nice place there. Then, I did the same thing again and re-mortgaged the place and moved into Clapham, again with Paul in tow.

Back then, I just bought at the advertised market price. Maybe I got a few thousand off, but not much. With my third house that I bought, I got £10,000 off the purchase price of a £200,000 flat and I thought that was the best negotiation that you could possibly do.

That was how I ended up owning three properties whilst still a lawyer and before I even turned thirty.

Property challenges

As I was still a lawyer while all this was going on, I was working all hours. I am not a DIY type of guy myself, so I got one of my friends, who was quite handy, to help me. He went around and looked after any things that needed fixing or maintaining.

I was the person who answered the phone calls and dealt with things if there was a big issue. I remember once one of the walls started cracking and falling down, so I had to get some structural supports fitted. I remember thinking, "Oh no! What do we do here?" I was quite hands on in the early days. You need to be at the beginning in the early stages, as you need to learn the ropes. It's great to have other people doing things for you, but it's good when you've also done it at one point yourself so you have the knowledge and understanding of what they are doing.

But as with most things, there will always be challenges. For example, with the place in Clapham that I bought, the previous owners had done an illegal sort of attic conversion. I bought it knowing that it was illegal and then I had to go to the planning department in the council and get retrospective planning permission. That was a real pain: it took about a year and it looked like it wasn't going to be approved at one point. I was worried I'd just have to lose this bedroom and close it off and make it attic space again. So, that was a big issue that I had to deal with. But it was nowhere near as time-consuming as being a full-time lawyer!

Law vs. property

All the time I was a lawyer, I was weighing up one life against the other: law versus property. What was interesting to me was that I was making more money from the real estate. That was blindingly obvious. I was earning a good salary working 12+ hour days as a lawyer. Then I was comparing this to the far greater paper profits coming in from real estate, putting in around four or five hours a week. So, for me that was a bit of an eye-opener actually seeing my net-worth go up. All the salary I was making as a lawyer was being spent on more expensive suits or a more expensive briefcase and expensive social events. Whereas with real estate, the money was staying there, not being spent, and increasing as the houses were going up in value. Yes, I did re-mortgage my properties every now and again, but when I did, the money was put into more real estate. So I could actually see my net-worth going up from relatively zero to a decent amount of money over the space of five years or so, as a result of investing in real estate.

Yes, I was working long hours, but I had my maintenance guy on hand to help me. I was in my twenties, and working hard as a lawyer is a badge of honour — it's not a bad thing, it's a good thing. I had no wife and kids to give me different priorities. Back then I was a working machine. That was pretty much what I did; I worked and I partied and I skied as much as I could.

The shift in my mindset

As I said, I just wanted a cool place to live with my first property. But with the successive properties, there was a shift in my mindset. I was looking for property where the finances stacked up and I didn't mind if it needed cosmetic work. I was happy to buy somewhere that wasn't brand, spanking, sparkly new, and I was happy to do a bit of painting and light renovations if necessary. The plan wasn't necessarily precise, as in, "I'll go in, spend £20,000 and it'll be worth an extra £25,000." At the end of the day, it was more about getting a decent property for the right price.

Back then, it was a piece of cake to get a mortgage. It seemed like you simply had to sign a piece of paper, and you got the finance. When I wanted to re-mortgage, it was exactly the same process. Mind you, this was before the crash, and I don't think anyone had ever sued a surveyor before 2008. Back then, it felt like surveyors would just say what you wanted them to say about the value of a property. Re-mortgaging was incredibly easy. I showed them my salary, they asked me how much I wanted, and that was that.

At that time, I didn't really know anybody else who was investing in property. The only people I knew who had more than one property were my friends who were decades older than me, who were rich, and who had places in the country. Take my old boss, for example — he had two homes: an estate in the country and a flat in London. But nobody else I knew was actively investing in real estate for the sake of building their wealth. There weren't any seminars or networking events back then; they just didn't exist in the 1990s and early 2000s. Very rich people, large financial institutions, developers—they were hosting events, but the private rented sector was just not organised nearly as much as it is today. There was nothing in England for folks like me who were interested in real estate. I just had to work it out for myself and ultimately, I had to go to North America to find out how to do it and copy their systems. Even the books about property investment and negotiation were primarily written by Americans.

"Financial freedom" wasn't really a phrase that was used in the UK back then. You hear it all the time today. But not then. Probably, the first time I really understood that concept was in one of the earliest books I read, *Rich Dad, Poor Dad,* by Robert Kyosaki. It's got some really simple financial concepts in it but back in the early 2000s, it was a real eye-opener to me. It was one of those books that all new investors should read. It has fantastic advice such as, "Buy an asset that puts money into your pocket every month and then over the long-term you'll get capital appreciation," and "Don't buy things that drain your pocket of money every month or go down in value." It wasn't rocket science, but it really changed my life when I read that.

I talked about it to my family and friends, but they were more focused on me being a lawyer. My parents always put real estate in the category of "just a little something he is doing on the side." They very much focused on me being a lawyer and working hard to be a lawyer. Even though I was making more money in real estate than I was as a lawyer, my inner circle couldn't see how the real estate was as important (or more important) than my being a lawyer. Law is a highly-regarded profession, and for most, that's a life goal. So many people have a goal to be, simply, a good professional, and to have job security for life. My grandma used to think that working for the council was the best thing that you could do because you got a job for life even if it paid peanuts.

Most people don't think about financial freedom, gaining wealth, and becoming a multi-millionaire.

SECTION 3

STARTING A PROPERTY BUSINESS

A classic Armistead Property bedroom

My arrival in Whistler

By the time I finally arrived in Whistler, I felt zero sense of apprehension, just excitement and adventure. Once I'd left my job, I'd done the hard bit. Walking out of the main door on the last day was relatively hard, but once that had been done, it had been done.

The first few days of being in Canada, the first few months, were very emotional. Even though I'd not done anything much – I'd just hopped on a plane – it was as though I'd achieved so much just getting out there.

Following my resignation, my next step was to get in touch with a Canadian realtor, an estate agent, to help me buy a place over there to live in. I began the process in the UK, then booked a flight over to Canada during the summer. I went for a week with half a dozen properties lined up to see. I had the finance already arranged, met the realtor, met the mortgage broker, and bought a small one-bedroom apartment in Whistler.

Most places here come furnished because it's quite hard having furniture delivered when you are under snow for six months of the year. It was a bog standard sort of an apartment and I could just pitch up with my rucksack and move in. One nice touch when I got there was seeing a brand new set of skis all wrapped up, sent from my close friends in England as a moving-in present. There was a sweet little note on there with something like, "Have a great time skiing. Here's to the rest of your life." They'd phoned up the local sports shop, bought a top-of-the-range pair of skis, and had them waiting for me. This was particularly special since I didn't take my skis over and had planned to buy a pair out there.

My first couple of weeks were amazing. They were better than I could possibly imagine. I missed my friends and my work colleagues, but I was still very much living the dream and reporting back to them. We'd e-mail each other and I'd tell people what was going on. It was before the days of Facebook so everything was still on e-mail.

I got out, I explored the area and did a lot of skiing. I also learnt to ski properly. I thought I was a semi-decent skier before I went to Whistler, but quickly realised I wasn't. The standard of skiing in Whistler is very, very high. It's a very athletic, outdoors community. I had an amazing experience exploring for the first few months. I also had a great time going around the village, meeting new people and getting to know them, people from all different walks of life.

I also got back in touch with the realtor again and began researching real estate in the Whistler area as well. That was one of the first things that I started doing, just trying to get to grips with Canadian culture. Even though they speak English over here, the culture is different. I needed to wrap my head around my new life.

My apartment was absolutely lovely and right in the middle of the village, and I knew it would be a good rental property after I'd finished with it, but for that particular period, it was a great place to live. In the process of changing continents and getting set up, I spoke to one of my good friends, who was a skier as well. He said he wanted to come over and spend a few months with me at the beginning. So, he and his girlfriend stayed in the bedroom of the apartment, and I stayed in the living room on the sofa bed. I had a little desk next to me. I used to get up early in the morning, do my work, and then every single day we went out skiing.

I'd bought that particular apartment because of its mountain views. Whistler is a glacier, so there's always snow at the very top of the mountain. Sometimes it's completely white, sometimes it's a mix of white and green. It depends on the seasons, but it changes, and one of the great things about nature is that you get a different view every day. Some days it's nice and sunny. If it's a nice July day and the sun's beating down, it's bright green, really lush green. Other times, when it's storming, you can barely see the mountain and everything is just white.

When I was a lawyer, I used to have a screensaver of a mountain on my computer, and then when I moved to the mountains, I figured I should make that the actual real view from my desk. Naturally, I set my desk up under the window. To this day, I've always had my desk facing the window over in Whistler, and there's always been a mountain view that I can just look up and see. Even if I glance up from work for just a couple of seconds, it's always worth it.

The Whistler lifestyle

Whistler, Canada is essentially a playground for adults. The company that owns the whole of the resort, puts a lot of money into the infrastructure. They don't just rely on private individuals setting a little chair lift here or a chair lift there. They'll go in and say, "Here's $100 million, let's develop that whole mountainside over there." As a result, it's one of the best outdoor meccas for skiing and biking in the world — at the very least, Whistler is probably the premier North American ski resort in winter time and the premier mountain biking mecca in summertime. We've got some amazing mountains and they're very useable mountains, mountains that you can run up or bike down, so consequently we get a lot of people coming up here and playing outdoors.

The heart of Whistler is comprised of a small community of about 10,000 people all year round. You get up to an extra 60,000 to 70,000 tourists on a busy day, so the village is very much dominated by tourism. It's a one-industry town that's been well-maintained and become quite affluent.

There is a huge nightlife scene with many bars and restaurants. I don't get involved in it these days as I'm now married with a couple of kids (I'm moving ahead of myself here; but we'll come to this later in my story!).

The stereotypical Canadian in Whistler tends to be very liberal and easygoing. If you've got your own little quirks, that's ok—you'll be accepted. They don't pigeonhole you like the Brits do. There's no class system over there. There's a bit of old money in Vancouver, and there are a few hillbillies, too. Overall, though, that sort of thing isn't important or noticed much there.

Another thing that isn't talked about much is work. I can go months and months without talking about work with my friends here. Certainly, if there's someone that you've been introduced to or if you're just having a natter with someone, work is not the topic of conversation like it is with most people in the UK. People don't tend to ask you, "How's work going?" or "What are you up to with work?" Everyone just assumes that work is work and it's going all right. Really, the important thing is: *What are you doing? What are you being? Have you done anything interesting? Have you been on any back country trips? Did you go biking today? Did you go for a run today?*" That's what people talk about — the big ticket, cool items that you're doing to actually properly enjoy yourself.

Canadians themselves tend to be very tolerant. They tend to be good at what they do, and they don't have the loud, brashness that Americans are famous for. Quite often I cannot tell the difference between a Canadian and an American accent, especially Americans from Washington State just below the border, but I can tell the difference in personality types instantly. You can usually tell an American from a Canadian just because of the way they behave. I like that. I like the fact that Canadians are half way between the Brits and the Americans.

There's loads of wildlife out here that you don't see in England. So, typically, I will see raccoons every day, and probably a bear every couple of days wandering through my back yard or out on the trails. I will see a bobcat or lynx probably once a week. The main predator out here that will cause humans some concern is the cougar. They're around, but you don't see them that often. In the rivers and streams there are loads of salmon. There are killer whales off the coast. Mountain animals like marmots are up in the alpine. There are many different types of animals over here. This is the main thing I love about Canada: it's an outdoor paradise.

50 properties in 50 months – the goal

At some point over the years, I was reading a book about setting and pursuing goals. The overriding principle was that you decided where you want yourself to be and then work backwards from that point, breaking it down into manageable chunks.

I wanted to be a real estate multi-millionaire, and I wanted to be an expert skier, so I figured to do both of those things, you needed a lot of property and a lot of time skiing on the slopes.

Now, according to that book whose title I've long since forgotten, that wasn't precise enough; I needed more precise and more achievable goals than that. Thus, I came up with the goal of skiing every month for 50 months and I figured that would be me skiing for about 200 days of the year, and buying an extra 50 properties, meaning that I would have generated at least an extra million in equity during that process.

Sure, the 50:50 was a bit of a gimmick, but behind it were some very solid and serious goals, which if I managed to stick to — skiing and buying property, monthly — would get me to my objectives.

My sense of purpose

Unlike some other folks, I don't have any deep, dark, driving, reasons to explain why I've wanted to pursue the life I've pursued. There are no negative forces from when I was a child. Yes, I did grow up in a relatively deprived area in East Manchester, and I certainly didn't want to stay in that sort of environment. But life wasn't going badly wrong for me and it wasn't as though I was getting myself into trouble with the police. In spite of the rough neighbourhood, I had a great childhood with two amazing and loving parents. I went to one of the best schools around, Manchester Grammar School, and this was very important in ensuring that I got into a good university and later on Law College.

The big why, for me, is not as important as accepting the fact that every now and again something comes along which to me is just an absolutely overriding passion and addiction. If I look and see that it's good, then I follow it and I go hard with it. If it's not such a good thing, then I keep half an eye on it. I do have a bit of an extreme personality.

I can recall my time as a lawyer when just thinking about skiing would raise my heartbeat. That passion became a sort of addiction: it was something that I absolutely had to do. I recognise that I'm not doing the world any good or curing cancer by going skiing; it's just purely for my life enjoyment and improvement. But for me, it was absolutely consuming.

Getting into real estate and building a successful real estate business became an overriding passion. It's akin to looking after your kids—it's that sort of feeling. When I have deep love and passion for something, when I'm positively addicted to something good, then I follow it to the extreme.

The skiing challenge

I was getting to be a decent skier and I wanted the adventure of taking my skiing all over the world. I wanted to go to Alaska and New Zealand and every skiing hotspot in between. All I needed to do was to go to these places. It would be expensive and I would have to make sacrifices, but it was going to be worth it to me.

I was moving along with my real estate goal simultaneously. In 2002, I bought eight properties. The following year, I decided to increase my purchases and buy twelve properties. It was during this period that I really began my real estate journey, and I was confident. I might not be able to buy a property every single month, but I felt certain that my goal, although a bit lofty, was manageable.

I needed to get well over 1,000 days skiing in as quickly as possible, which was why I chose the 50:50 challenge. I hit skiing hard. There were several years where I did over 200 days of skiing, which is a phenomenal amount. Not many people in the world do that amount of skiing, and I did get myself up to a level I was very happy with.

Skiing and real estate investment were probably split in time and importance at that stage. My goal of becoming an excellent skier was up there alongside setting up a successful property business. In Whistler, I ski alongside guys that have grown up skiing. These are people that were born on skis who have done over 100 days of skiing every year. I wasn't necessarily competing with them — these guys were my friends — but I knew that I had to get up to their level. So I clearly needed to spend a lot of time on the slopes. Skiing was not just a reward; skiing was the reason why I moved to Whistler.

My way of making this new lifestyle work was to get up really early in the morning. So I started a pattern of getting up at between 3 a.m. and 4 a.m., which was 11 a.m. UK time. I would work for several hours until the end of the UK working day, and then I would go skiing afterwards. In the early evening, I'd do more research and then go to bed early. So that became my new routine of working UK hours whilst working remotely and also getting the skiing in at the same time. That's a routine I still maintain all these years later!

I threw myself into my business and my skiing, heart and soul. And I worked hard, which I've found to be the bottom line underlying pretty much everything I've ever accomplished. There was a lot of hard work that went into my business: networking, meeting people, befriending estate agents, finding deals, talking to all sorts of people. I managed to find the properties, get the deals, do the deals.

And though 50 properties in 50 months may sound like a gimmick, I completed on the last property about two or three days before the 50 months expired. So I did do it, but only just barely. It was a close call.

Getting focused

With the 50:50 challenge, the question I'm frequently asked is: "How do you fit all of that in — skiing and viewing all these properties and doing the deals — when there's only so many hours in a day?"

That was the challenge. I didn't want to make it an easy challenge. I could have just done 50 months of skiing or 50 properties and let the other thing look after itself. These were the two things I really wanted: to become a millionaire through real estate and to become world-class skier, and I couldn't wait to do either of them; they had to be done at the same time. That was directly after I left law, so I had a year of sorting myself out and setting things up and then that was my goal: the 50:50 challenge.

I did a lot of work, I did a lot of skiing, and survived off of relatively little sleep. I wasn't a well-rounded guy back then, but I was very focused on working and skiing.

Back then, I did everything concurrently: training in real estate investment and looking at properties. I still do it this way today. I didn't just do real estate investment training and then go and buy properties based on that training. I was actively looking for real estate and reading as many books as I possibly could get my hands on. I did a ton of research, and at the same time I was looking for different properties and trying to research different business plans, and look at different areas to invest in. At this point, I didn't have my own business plan fully developed, but I was working out what type of business plan I wanted, and how it was all going to work. It was a work in progress.

In the early days, I was a sponge for new information, learning a ton about income-producing properties. I remember going on a property investment course where people were focused on buying a property below market value and having it so that it put money into your pocket every single month. If you had a property making you £100 a month, and you had 20 of those, you've got £2,000 a month coming in. That's what a lot of people were aiming for. They were trying to get cash-flow so they could turn property into a proper business. Whereas before, in London, I had just looked at how much the value of a property increased because of market forces and capital appreciation.

After I moved to Canada, I came across people that were using property to pay for their living expenses every single month and they were also adding value to and making money from the properties like that. The capital appreciation side of things was a bonus. These were investors, not speculators.

TOP TIP: MAKE SURE YOUR CASH FLOW IS POSITIVE.

You don't know when the market is going to go up, but you do know if your mortgage costs are £500 and you're making £600 a month from rent, you've got £100 of surplus. You also know that if you buy a property for £1 and you do certain well-considered renovations for another £1 then your property won't just be worth £2 — it could be worth £3. So, they were treating real estate as a business, which you could work on and increase the value, rather than just sitting there and letting the market forces do the work for you.

Back then, the UK was a long way behind North America when it came to real estate investment. The only landlords that I'd ever come across before I went to Canada were just amateurs, so to see the business that I had sort of fallen into being done in a professional way was impressive. I was meeting some really inspiring people. I sat next to this guy at a conference and he had a couple of hundred apartments. I said, "Wow, that's amazing. You must be some sort of rock star." He looked at me, shook his head and just laughed, "Nowhere near. I'm getting by; I'm making a living out of it. But, no." he pointed and said, "The people over there have done tens of thousands." I can just remember thinking, "How on earth can you do that? That's just massive," because they weren't companies; they were just normal everyday people that were doing these things. So, this was the power of treating real estate as a business, not just as an asset class.

> **TOP TIP:** PROPERTY IS NOT JUST A PASSIVE ASSET CLASS, IT'S A BUSINESS.

Your network is your net worth

I went to loads of networking events and my business developed because of my networking. I looked at different areas to buy in and different business plans, and I ended up taking my chosen route really because of one mentor who was a good, honest guy who took me under his wing. We would go out for drinks and meals together and I spent nights at his house. We used to stay up for hours talking about real estate and finance. He was one of the key cornerstones of my networking and then my "power team" as I now call it.

I really got started by copying his business plan. When I outgrew it, I changed it and made it a more high-end version of what he does, but it's the same sort of business plan. So, the networking was absolutely key and that's how my business turned into what it is today.

I'm assuming that you're reading this book either because you're interested in how I was able to set up my Nomad-lifestyle business or because you're keen to do something similar yourself. So I'll give you a few tips that I wish I'd known when I got started ...

Networking Tips

1. Don't hog people.
   I will go and if I see a room full of people I'll think, "Okay, I'll maybe speak to everyone for two to five minutes." If I talk to someone I find interesting, I'll take their card and pass mine over. I usually do that with most people anyway, but if it's someone interesting, I'll take their business card and I put it in a separate pocket or in my wallet. That way, I separate the wheat from the chaff, so to speak. I usually start by asking them about themselves. It's usually someone's favourite topic of conversation! I will never be arrogant and I'll never be nervous. I won't think that I'm a better developer or investor than someone or I'll never think that someone's better than me. Just because they've got more or less properties or money, it doesn't matter. It's people meeting people at the end of the day. I don't really try to sell myself; in fact, I never try to sell anything at a meeting. I just want to try to find out what people are doing and if there's anything interesting there, then I'll follow it further.

2. Ask, don't tell
   Asking about them, rather than telling about me, is key. Then, if I like someone, I'll offer them something. For example, over the last six months, I've been going to

networking events. Our business, Armistead Property, won the UK Property Awards Renovation prize — a prestigious award. So, when I'm talking to people and if I like them and if they're doing a similar type of thing to me I'll say, "You might be interested in this. I'm not trying to sell you an apartment or anything, but if you're interested in seeing how our business works, then we've just won the UK Renovation Award and I can take you around that site if you wish. It's a lovely block of 16 apartments, a boutique development in an old mansion house a couple of miles outside Manchester. If you're interested, I'll take you around and give you a tour for half-an-hour or so." Half of the people that I talk to take me up on that offer, simply because it sounds fun. If they're into real estate and doing developments, chances are they'll want to see it. So, I give rather than ask for things.

3. Look for the spark

    You're looking for a spark; you're looking to see if you might be able to work with someone in the future. The two things that real estate investors are always looking for is more deals and more money. In my business, there are always problems. There are some good problems to have, and there are some less good ones. We need to make sure we have enough workers to do the job. We need to know quantity surveyors, we need to know who's lending money at the moment etc., etc. So anything that I can pick up from someone else is welcome and good. Everyone's out there working at the coalface, getting their hands dirty, so it's good to hear other investors' experiences. I'm never in a needy situation these days. I never go to a networking event saying, "My God, I need an extra £100,000 to do this deal or else it's the end for me." You should never put yourself in that position, and you should never come across as desperate. Yet, I always want to do business and I always want to take ideas from people and share my ideas.

4. Know how to network
   Go around finding out people's top tips and sharing your own so you're all getting there faster. You're all sharing things like, "This bank manager was really good and this one wasn't. This mortgage broker wasn't so good…"

A lot of newbies—most people in a room at a networking event, really—are out there to try and borrow money from you to do a deal because that's what they're lacking. That is not the case with me, nor is it the case for other investors who have been in the industry for a while. We've got money, we've got deals; we could always do with more money, we could always do with more deals, but it's not the end of the world if that networking event doesn't throw up something like that. Quite often, I'm talking to someone for a couple of minutes and they'll say, "Okay, well, it looks like you've got a great team. I've got this house, under an option. I'm looking for a builder to do it up and someone to lend me the money. Would you want to do it up and lend me the money?" There's no way I'm going to do that kind of business with anyone within two minutes. It takes three or four proper face-to-face meetings before you would trust anyone to go into business with them; either borrowing money from them or lending them money. So, with me networking's a slow burn, but the quickest thing you can get out of it is working out what other people are doing, sharing your top tips with them, and getting top tips back from them.

> **TOP TIP:** KEEP ON LEARNING. ALWAYS KEEP SHARPENING
> THE SAW.

My action plan

My first action plan lasted about two or three years. It looked fantastic on paper and I got it from reading many, many different books about strategy.

My underlying principle was that you invest/buy real estate in three different property cycles that are operating separately and will accomplish three different things. So, mine turned out to be London (where I already had property), a ski resort in a foreign country (which turned out to be Whistler, Canada) and then income-producing properties in the North of England (a totally different asset class to London) though I didn't know where that place in the North of England was going to be.

So, with three different cycles, at any one time, two of them will be doing well and one will be doing not so well. Rents might be going up in two places and not going up in another place, but overall you hedge your bets and the strategy works—that was the theory.

Now that's okay if you've got a handful of properties, but you can't really manage many properties like that without it being a lot harder and a lot more time-consuming.

That was my original business plan, which eventually evolved into the business plan that I have today. The cornerstone of that was my third area (income-producing properties in the North of England). After extensive research I eventually focused on Manchester, and in particular South Manchester. This seemed to be the most promising area to me. It had the best mix of a good tenant base and demand, strong rents, and good potential capital appreciation. Starting in 2002, I bought my first couple of places there. The focus on South Manchester however really cemented itself from 2004 onwards.

When I first met my old mentor he had a business plan of having all his properties in one postcode. His idea was very much the same as

Warren Buffet's idea of putting all your eggs in one basket, but making sure it's a brilliant basket. He had many apartments in blocks of flats (usually old Victorian properties). He would own the whole block (10 or 20 units in one house), all in the M20 postcode, which is Didsbury in South Manchester. He had a couple of hundred units spread out around Didsbury like that. He knew every single road, he knew every estate agent there, he knew where the underground rivers were. He knew where the restrictive covenants were, the layouts of buildings before he'd even been into them. He was an absolute local expert; no one could beat him for Didsbury. He was the world's best real estate investor in Didsbury, and you had better believe that he got access to all the juicy deals because of it. He was in a great position. He used to sit there, wait for his phone to ring and the agents would literally give him deals.

I realised the merit of that so that was the business plan that I copied. I wanted to make myself the world's expert in an area, and I chose the postcode next door to him: M21, which is Chorlton. That's what I am today. I'm now my version of my mentor back in the day. So, he was the best investor in Didsbury and I set out to become the best investor/developer in Chorlton.

> **TOP TIP:** FIND YOUR NICHE AND FOCUS ON IT. BECOME THE BEST IN THE WORLD AT WHAT YOU DO. YOU WILL MAKE MORE MONEY AND GET MORE OPPORTUNITIES THAT WAY. BECOME A SPECIALIST — THIS WILL GIVE YOU AN AMAZING COMPETITIVE ADVANTAGE.

Finding my investment areas

It took tons of research to pick my investment area. Firstly, I had to assess the market value of different types of real estate and their respective rents. Next up was determining the closeness to transport links, hospitals, universities and finding out which local councils were being progressive and which were not. I had various checklists and I went all over the country. I went to Liverpool, Birmingham, Manchester; I went up to Paisley just outside of Glasgow, I looked at little terraced houses in Wales, new builds in Leeds, and workers' cottages in Yorkshire.

The places that ticked all the boxes for me, and that I got a good feel for, included the postcodes for Whalley Range and Chorlton. They were slightly different places, but they're next door to each other. The rents were good; they were up and coming areas. Chorlton had already come up years prior. Whalley Range was up and coming and still is. It's slightly edgier than Chorlton, but still a place you'd like to be. It has some beautiful properties, and most importantly some very big buildings. Many of them were very beautiful externally, but old and unloved, and they'd all been subject to some very old-school business plans like HMOs and shared accommodation, but generally done to a low standard.

I realised I could focus on buying these places at what I thought was a cheap price, splitting them into proper apartments — nice, London-style, high-end apartments that I would live in when I was a lawyer — and then splitting the title up from freehold into leasehold. I could keep the freehold, selling some of the leaseholds, or keep and re-mortgage them. There's money in all of the various stages there.

Those types of properties don't exist commonly in England or Wales. For example, when I went over to Wales, I was just looking at terraced houses, and there's a limit to what you can do to those. It's the same in Scotland as well: they had terraced houses and they're big terraced houses, but primarily terraced houses. The buildings in Manchester were big and I knew that I could fit between five and twenty apartments in a lot of them, so there was the potential to produce something quite smart and profitable. Not many people were doing this, but there was definitely a demand for it.

Over the years, I realized that I got quite lucky with my choice of location. Manchester has got the most progressive city council in the UK and they are aggressively regenerating the city centre with building work. I'm sure that in my lifetime it will be one of the big success stories of urban regeneration and one of the premier cities in Europe.

You can learn a lot also by the places I considered but discarded. I went to Liverpool and to East Manchester, and I looked around areas where on paper it looked fantastically good and you could get really good yields (around 8-9 per cent, sometimes more). I remember waiting to enter a property in an area of Liverpool and some people who were just hanging around on the street corner were just glaring at me in a "What are you doing around here?" kind of way. After touring the property, it didn't take long to get a feel for the area and realise it was the type of place where if you wanted all of your rent money you'd have to go and get it with a baseball bat, and that wasn't the game I wanted to be in!

The property owner was a big, gruff character and I remember thinking, "Okay this is not for me. I want to deal with a certain tenant type. I want to deal with someone that will respect a property." I wanted to own blocks of 10 to 20 apartments. I didn't want one troublesome tenant in there annoying all the others; it would just rapidly go downhill. For example, in Liverpool in the house that I looked after, there were burn marks in the carpet. The tenant had been lying in bed smoking and putting her cigarettes out on the carpet. You didn't want to be doing business with people like that.

People like that don't care about paying on time (or at all), especially if they're strung out on drink or drugs.

I wanted to deal with professional people, yet I still wanted an area that had a good return on it. So, the high yields that I could have gotten in Liverpool chipped down to 5-6% in South Manchester: Whalley Range and Chorlton. Why did I choose these areas? I knew these people had jobs and that they would pay the rent. I decided to focus on the higher end of the tenant demographic.

Chorlton and Whalley Range

Chorlton has a lot of young professional people living there. There's a little bit of left-wing edginess going on. We've got a corner shop in Chorlton that I think sells more Guardians than any other corner shop in the UK, and we're proud of the fact. You can buy 12 different types of quinoa down at the local deli and multiple flavours of hummus! It definitely has a Brighton type of feel to it. It is respectable and desirable in an artsy, bohemian type of way. There's a high percentage of university-educated people and lots of people in education, and you're surrounded by academics, lecturers, school teachers, maybe post-grads or teachers at the university. There are very few chain stores there. We do have a McDonalds, an M&S and a Costa Coffee, but most of Chorlton is filled with small, independent shops. We have got the best bakers I've ever seen, the best butchers, and the best fishmongers. You can walk about with your little hemp bag and go to the butchers and then the next shop you go to is your fruit and veg shop. I myself also have a home there. I could have a home anywhere in Manchester but I choose to have one in the middle of Chorlton. It's beautiful. I love the fact that my local is a little tapas bar with eight tables, a great atmosphere, and authentic, great food (everyone there is a native Spanish speaker).

It's not a secret; everyone who's earning decent money in Manchester wants to live in Chorlton or Didsbury. You have more chain bars in Didsbury. You see more lawyers and accountants about, lots of people wearing ties in Didsbury. In Chorlton, there's more media types. When the BBC relocated to Manchester, the staff flocked to Chorlton en masse and not Didsbury.

Whalley Range is a bit rougher and readier. It's a bit edgier than Chorlton, but it's still a nice, desirable place to be. We have areas of Manchester that are very deprived areas and you wouldn't want to go there alone, let alone live there. Places with tons of unemployment, lots of people underperforming, and not working, or working part-time. Whalley Range is nothing like that, but it's cheaper price-wise and rental-wise than Chorlton. The houses in Chorlton tend to be beautiful red brick houses, whereas Whalley Range has some really nice, very big, grand manor homes. Back in the day, that was where the merchants lived in the 1800s. This is when all the big houses were built in Whalley Range and then the workers used to live in Chorlton in the smaller houses. So they're two really nice, enjoyable places to do business, with a good mix of housing stock.

Long-distance investing

You often hear advice at property seminars which goes along the lines of: "I wouldn't invest in somewhere that is more than an hour to drive to." You may therefore think it's strange that I decided to invest in Manchester rather than Canada.

Why would I invest somewhere that was a 24-hour journey door to door, involving twelve hours of flying? Of course it's a lot easier to manage your business if you've got all of your properties within a half-hour drive of you. But it doesn't mean that you necessarily have to live there. Yes, it is a negative to live so far away from your business, but there are lots of ways in which I make it work. For example, I now employ my own building team of twenty full-time builders, and use the same suppliers that give us very good discounts, and I've got maintenance guys that just go around that I employ full-time. I own over 100 properties in just two postcodes: M16 and M20. If we had those 100 properties scattered all over the UK and had to employ people separately, the time spent doing that would really cut into my working day and you'd be having to pay everyone an extra 20-30 per cent profit margin because you don't have the economies of scale there. In one sense, I have a very local business, even though it's managed remotely.

I have thought about investing in Canada of course. But that's not my business plan. It's a totally different game over here. It's even a different construction: everything is built with wood. All the building regulations are different. Apartment blocks in Whistler don't really exist. You couldn't do what I want to do over there.

The shift in mindset

When I was viewing properties, the ratio of viewings to deals going through was about 100-1. I would view 100 properties for every property I would buy. I'd typically look online or through estate agents' leaflets at 100 properties, 10 of which I would view, three of which I put offers in on, and one of which I would buy.

Now, there are many properties in my area that I've seen, I've been inside, and that I know. I've almost certainly been inside at least one house on every single street in my two postcodes. I know the properties and the area like the back of my hand.

In the early days of setting up my business, there were times where I felt I was pipped to the post by other people — quite disheartening when you are trying to build up your business and your reputation.

I lost deals, people outbid me, but you just have to think, "This happens. There's a lot of deals out there." It's always frustrating if there's something you want and someone beats you to it, but at the end of the day it's like buses: there will always be another deal.

There's no point in feeling bad about something that you can't do anything about. If it was a mistake on my part – for example, if I was negotiating too low and it was a strong market – then I need to take that one on the chin and think, "Okay don't be so hard with the negotiating next time. The market's moving quickly. Let's get it done at the full asking price if I know I can make a profit margin on it."

One of my main challenges when I first set up a business in Manchester being operated from Whistler was switching gear from my old "job" mindset. Not reporting back to someone and not being given work was a very big change. I had to work out what I wanted, how to get there, what work I should be doing. I remember at one point I was spending a huge amount of time doing research and looking at things; I was spending days and days on researching and analysis. I knew it was all worthwhile, but it wasn't making me money. I would go off on tangents thinking, "It might be good to work out what the Brazilian economy was doing 20 years ago and seeing if there's a parallel to what's happening in Whistler today." I had to have a little sticker on my computer screen at one point, saying, "Is this making you money?" I would keep on looking back at it and think, 'That's the bottom line isn't it? You know, it doesn't really matter what happened in the economy 20 years ago. It's more important to try and find a property that I can pay a mortgage plus costs of £500 and rent out for £600. Let's focus a little bit, Peter. You need to find a property deal in the next couple of months and that's what you should be focused on."

So, there was a very different mindset to adjust to. It was great being a lawyer and getting all the training, but it was also very limiting. As a lawyer you can't be 80% right. If you're 80% right you could be wrong. As a lawyer you have to give advice as close to 100% as you possibly can and if there is a couple of percent you are unsure about, then you have to qualify that and say so. At the end of the day, it was also up to the client to act. Lawyers don't push the button. They are advice providers on the whole.

You can never be 100 per cent sure in real estate. You've got to operate on 80 per cent certainty most of the time, and that was a hard shift in mindset for me to take. So, suddenly having to decide, "Okay I will buy your property for £100,000. Let's do it," was difficult. Real estate's always a big money game. So it was hard committing so much money on a deal that I might not be absolutely certain as to whether it would make "x" or "y" amount at the end of the day.

However, every single one of my deals has made money and I've done in nearly 500 property deals since I started out.

Another challenge I had initially was feeling like I needed more training. When I was a lawyer, for example, I did university for three years, then Law College for two years, then I started earning money and got sponsored through Law College. Then I spent two years doing articles. So, it was a serious process to go through. I hadn't had anywhere near that level of training in property when I first started out.

Building relationships with estate agents

One of the important things I did to build my business was to work on building my relationships with estate agents.

There are no short-cuts there. The tried and tested way is doing good business with them. So, you do a deal with them, you prove that you're a good person, you don't mess them about, you don't BS them, you do what you say, and then you treat them well during the whole process — get them a present afterwards. The more times you do that, the more they know it's worth favouring you, as they know that you'll do a deal.

They want to sell property. They're looking for guys who don't mess about. They want someone who isn't going to renegotiate the price again after it's been agreed, just because there's a slight damp problem that's brought up in a survey. They don't want any last-minute shenanigans. They want to deal with someone who is a good person to deal with. It takes time to build up good working relationships. There are no shortcuts. It's just a case of being a good, honourable, solid businessperson and not messing people about.

> **TOP TIP:** PROPERTY IS A RELATIONSHIPS GAME. BUILD GOOD RELATIONSHIPS.

One of my biggest success principles is honouring a deal.

I rarely have a deal fall through. It takes me a while to agree a deal, and to make sure I've got all my bases covered. Once this has been done, I'm on the hook: my reputation is at stake and I'm committed. So if I agree to do something, it's important that I follow through with it. Every now and again, the person selling to me backs out of a deal and there's nothing I can do about that. If it's from my end, I don't back out, and I don't let deals fall down.

> **TOP TIP:** DO WHAT YOU SAY AND DON'T BS OR OVER-COMMIT. IF YOU BREAK YOUR WORD, YOU ARE DEAD IN THIS GAME.

Doing your due diligence

I've never bought a property without viewing it or without viewing most of the rooms in it. I view almost everything that I buy personally. However, quite often, there are apartments that we cannot get into because the tenant just won't let us in.

I did not have a good handle on building work when I first started my business. I'm not a practical person: I spent my childhood and teens just studying and working hard academically. I was a lawyer; I'm just not a practical guy full-stop. Early on, when I first started to invest in Manchester, I realised that I needed a good handyman or builder. So I found a builder who helped me get a handle on costs, working out what we should be looking for.

I worked with him for about five years or so and we grew a professional building team slowly but surely. The very high quality building team that we managed to get was key to our property development, both during the early period and, very importantly, during the recession when things started becoming more difficult. We were pretty much the only developers in the area that were able to carry on building and developing during that time.

Financing my property deals

Before 2008 was a golden age for mortgages, especially 2004-2007. I was absolutely fine borrowing money from banks and using creative no-money-down techniques to increase the amount of deals I could do. The bog standard buy-to-let mortgage was pretty much all you needed. That was the area that everyone was focusing on and it was easy to buy properties at a relatively high loan-to-value rate, it was also relatively easy to put in a little bit of money and then draw it out very quickly, sometimes even on the same day you bought the property.

I would buy a property, putting in say £10,000 of my own money in the morning. Then, by the evening when my solicitor had completed the deal, I'd be pulling back £8,000 or £9,000 from the initial £10,000. During this period, it was very easy to build up a portfolio very quickly as long as you had a relatively high, risk tolerance and you didn't mind borrowing pretty much all the money to buy a property. I was buying a pound's worth of property for 80p. If I mortgaged all of that 80p, I still had my 20p profit margin lying in there. That was my business plan.

Before the credit crunch, it was very easy to do creative finance deals, so I became an absolute master at it. The mortgage companies knew how these were done — they allowed them to be done — and there were various strategies available at the time that enabled me to buy real estate very quickly with none of my own money. For instance, in 2003, I bought a block of eight flats on a credit card — that's right, a *credit card*. That's where the money came from. I did not put any money in apart from what I'd borrowed on the credit card, and at the end of the transaction, the credit card was fully paid off. I had money back in my pocket after I'd refinanced it all and it was cash flowing positively. That was legal and accepted at the time, but not any more.

People still do similar things today. These strategies were all sanctioned and approved by the banks back then, whereas now they definitely do not approve of them. I still talk to people who are using these strategies, though I think if they got found out they might be in a lot of trouble.

When the recession came along things changed dramatically (as I'll discuss in later chapters). I quickly realised that my pot of money wasn't going to stretch forever, so I started using joint venture partnerships to finance my projects, especially when the banks stopped lending after the credit crunch. That then became the preferred way of doing business. Before 2008, there were quite a few creative techniques that you could use to buy property with no money down. After 2007, those techniques became either almost impossible to do or illegal. Some people still do them today, but they're breaking the law or the mortgage rules. So, that's when I made my own change and started doing more joint ventures.

These days, you need to put down many times more than before the recession. You need a lot more cash up front, and that tends to be done by investors pooling their resources. People that are cash rich and time poor quite often collaborate with real property investors that are out there in the trenches finding deals, yet who do not necessarily have the £60,000 to £70,000 per property that they need to put down to finance the deal.

Setting up my own lettings agency

I hesitated. I thought about it, but at the time, the figures were relatively clear. I was paying a letting agent £60,000 per annum to manage my properties at the time. If I employed a full-time lettings agent to work solely for me, paid them £20,000 and put £10,000 into extra marketing, then that was £30,000 per annum, so I could reduce my costs by half. That was a good business decision. I needed to work out how it was done, but that's how every business in the UK operates. You phone up your accountant, you tell them what they're doing, they set up the PAYE for you, you get some branded corporate cards and some proper letterheads — these were all things that other people had done and that's exactly what I needed to do.

It was new territory though. Most people that I knew, had not done this. My mentors managed over 100 properties themselves as one-man bands. I looked at them and thought, 'That's a very good, sexy business there, which they've built up over the years. They really control the costs, and everything looks great with it." But I wanted to take it a step further than that and I recognised that setting up the structure and having a system in place was the way to do that. I was very happy to contract to bring that in-house sooner rather than later and get the system going. I could manage all the properties myself, especially remotely, and more staff made perfect sense.

SECTION 4

THE NOMAD LIFESTYLE

Create a great neutral blank canvas for the buyer, then add wow factor with the dressings

The Nomad office

Moving around a lot means I have learned to use my car as my office. There are certain things you can do to make your working day run more smoothly and efficiently, and to also make things easier on yourself.

If I know that I've got meetings, for example, I will put a couple of bottles of water in the car, a whole bunch of snack food (such as nuts and dates), a recharger for my phone (always in the car), and a briefcase with files for the four or five different properties I will inevitably be visiting. I will go around the various properties, speak to people and go to my lawyer with the files in there. My car in Manchester is a mobile office for me and I have it kitted out with all my gear.

There are pros and cons of course. When I'm in Manchester, I need to be out and about doing meetings and one of the most important things that I do is what I commonly call "kissing frogs." I will take a lot of people out for cups of coffee during the day or beers in the evening and talk to them. It often goes nowhere, but face-to-face meetings are a key part of business; you just need to do that. So, me being able to be out and about rather than stuck in an office the whole time is really helpful.

I want the right people in Chorlton and Whalley Range to see my face and know that I'm around and actively doing business. Because I'm in Canada and physically not around for a lot of the time, I make a special effort to meet people when I'm back. I want to be out and about shaking people's hands, and building up personal relationships. I want to be going on site and seeing the build and making sure that the builders are happy and they know what they're doing. The paperwork can usually wait until I'm back in my office in Whistler.

I have a traditional office in Manchester as well. I have a room in the office with the rest of my staff, but during the day, I almost never use it. I use it early in the morning, for three or four hours before other people arrive, then chances are I go to meetings straight away. I'm out for most of the day in the meetings and then I get back around late afternoon/early evening and see the people in the office for a little while, and then after they go home and I've got the office to myself for a few hours.

Building my team

I have deliberately chosen people better than me to do jobs in my business. I often joke that, "There's one amateur in my business and that's me!" That's because I make sure that every person I employ is brilliant at their job.

So, I have a head of building, I have a head maintenance guy, a head of the property rental side. I trust these people totally. I don't check up on them, but they report to me. Every week I get a written report; there's a format for it. Every single property that we own is itemised. There are various sections for maintenance, for rentals, etc. So, if I need to check what's being done, I can check it. Do I have absolute certainty that the cleaner goes around once every month to a particular property? Not necessarily. I have that certainty because my head of property management, Sean, tells me that's happening, and I trust him as I would trust a family member because that's the way that we operate.

I employ amazing people to do jobs in the business which I can't do. I'm not the type of businessperson that monitors and micro-manages. Some business leaders are very hands-on. I'm not like that. Richard Branson has a very hands-off business style, so does Warren Buffett; they pick really good people to manage their businesses for them. They set up or finance the businesses and maybe grow them; they do the high-level strategic thinking, but the management of the business is left to other more capable people. I try to adopt the same principle as well. I want to work on my business, not in it.

> **TOP TIP:** WORK WITH PEOPLE WHO ARE BETTER THAN YOU.

In the past, I've made mistakes and I've learned from them. I've hired a couple of people that were not trustworthy. I had one builder that I hired who used to sleep on the job... literally! He used to go round to our empty rental properties on the pretense of doing a job and just sleep in the properties. It became obvious he wasn't doing his job as it would take an hour to do the gardening yet he'd come back two and a half hours later and the job was done badly. So, he got picked up on it and quizzed and he said, "No, no, no. It was just a rough gardening day. There was a lot of work to be done." Then someone went round to check up on him doing another garden, and found him sleeping in a bed. He'd just curled himself up, took his boots off and was having an hour's kip on my clock. So, I have had occasional comedy situations where people have abused my trust. But on the whole, the normal way that I operate is to trust people, but to verify. The principle is: trust with verification.

In general, I've been very lucky with my staff. I've employed people that I know of already and have seen to be trustworthy and hardworking. I've actively poached people. If there's someone who I think is good at their job (and I've done this with several property managers) I will actively go and say, "I like you — you're really good at your job. If you're ever thinking about moving, give me a call won't you?"

I leave most of the hiring and firing decisions for the builders down to the head builders. They know their job; they know what they're doing and getting involved with. For office staff, I've always hired people that I have a good personal rapport with, as well as being able to do the job – people that I would enjoy sitting in an office with every day, because my business is my baby. It's my name on the front door at the end of the day.

During a job interview, you ask lots of questions and it becomes obvious if someone isn't suitable. I was interviewing a man once, but it became very clear that he didn't know how to use a computer. All he could use was Facebook, he couldn't use Word or Excel. He said, "I could probably learn" and the way he said it wasn't a, "Yeah, I can pick that up if I need to. I can learn it." It was a half-hearted, "Oh, I don't really want to..." And in today's age where we're all networked up and we're all downloading things from the cloud!

I'm in Manchester then Canada. My main guys live in Madrid and Poland and also commute to work and work remotely. Everyone relies on the computers, Skype, the Internet and mobile phones. You need to be computer/Internet savvy to be able to get things done. The interviewee clearly wasn't that person. That was blindingly obvious. He was a nice guy and could probably do a good part of the job, but he wouldn't have fitted in with my business.

Family culture

My business has what I call a family culture and I think this has been a big part of my success. Let me take you back to how it all started. In 2002, I met two Polish brothers, Stefan and Michael, and they started working for me full-time. They brought their families up to Manchester – one had a family in London and the other had a girlfriend in Poland. We were working with each other every single day very closely. At first they renovated a few small properties for me, and now they head up the whole of the development/ construction side of the business and have 20-30 builders working under them.

Back in the day I was very hands-on. Very quickly, within a couple of years, those guys became like family. I gave them full access to the credit card and all the bank accounts and bought them a van. I gave them an apartment each to live in. I lent them the money for their first car and the deposit for their first house, all within a couple of years. They, from their side, have worked tirelessly in our business now for 16 years and have produced some truly amazing and unbeatable award-winning properties.

That's really when the family ethos started. We used to go out for drinks and meals together (and still do!). It became more than just business. This then set the tone for the way I worked with and treated my team.

Finding the deals

Around about this stage, buy-to-let investments were becoming more mainstream and there were more property investor meetings and landlord conferences cropping up. I went to as many of those as I possibly could whenever I was in the UK, meeting as many investors as I could. About two-thirds of my deals came through personal contacts with old-school landlords that wanted to get rid of their rundown properties. They were looking at retiring or just putting their money somewhere else. I would talk to them and do off-market deals. So networking the old-fashioned, traditional way accounted for my biggest supply chain. Of course, it was also important to get into the estate agents' good books and to let everyone know that we were in the business of buying properties. But at the end of the day, it's all about talking to people and building personal relationships.

I got one of my most profitable deals, which was a portfolio of buildings, through the furniture delivery guy, who knew that we were always looking for deals. One day he said that he knew of a landlord who was talking about selling up. I got in touch and ended up buying dozens of properties over the course of a few years from that one particular landlord. It was all about old-fashioned networking, pounding the streets, and answering my phone when it rang.

Now I have a full-time property sourcer that works for me. When I first started my business, I did everything. Then, as the business developed and grew, the things that I could contract out I did contract out, slowly but surely. The first thing to go was the property management and the lettings side of things. I passed those over to a lettings agent initially, then after I got maybe 20 to 30 properties it was more cost effective for me to employ my own lettings agent in-house. I just farmed out the jobs that either I wasn't good at or that I didn't like doing, and I concentrated on the jobs which were more important to the business: the ones that had the biggest financial impact.

Learning to manage a team of staff

I'd come from a big firm when I was a lawyer and I worked quite closely with the people in the HR department. It was a company with over 1,000 people, and I saw how they handled things professionally. I saw how the reporting structures worked — for example, how I used to report to my boss. So I mimicked their strategies: how they dealt with HR and the reporting structures.

It's not time-consuming or complicated. It's easy to fill out, but it is detailed. We have set ways that everyone in the company reports back up the pyramid and it works well. Yes, we do get bad eggs every now and again. I've had to sack people. That's more common on the building side. Building is hard work and people have to work really hard and put their hearts and souls into it. Sometimes people just don't cut it.

I've sacked people in the past, both in the office and on the building side of things. It's one of the areas of my business that I enjoy the least. I am probably a bit guilty of leaving bad people in place for too long and trying to help them change and make them better workers than they are.

I am very influenced by my reading of the classic Dale Carnegie book, *How to Win Friends and Influence People*, the gist of which is to praise people and tell them that they're doing a good job — it brings out the best side of them. It's good advice and works 90 per cent of the time, but not always. I can remember with one particular staff member I was having problems with. I tried the Carnegie approach, and while the approach is usually effective, if you have a person who's not suited to that job or maybe not even suited to hard work (there are people like that about) the encouragement won't work. I tried giving him ego boosts, telling him he was doing a great job, suggesting ways he could do an even better job — but it didn't work. I kept him in the business for way too long. I should have cut ties with him a year or two before I did.

Right now, we have not had to sack anyone in the office for eight years. I have some amazing people in there. When you have amazing people, make sure you treat them well. We pay them way above normal wages. We tell them they're doing a good job, because they are. We create a good working environment for them. It works the same on our building side: we don't have people leaving us for more money or better working conditions — that never happens.

People like gestures that show that you respect them for their work. So I treat my team well financially, however money only goes so far and there are other parts of the equation as well. People need to feel valued and that their time is being spent in the right way. It's important to work out what is important to the individuals and to respect and honour that. For example, I make sure that my two head builders do not have a set amount of holiday time. They can take what holiday they want, whenever they want, as long as they finish the job and make it work between them. It's their decision as to how much holiday time they take.

There are now three great guys that run the building side of my business. The two original brothers (who have been joined by their younger brother Matthew) have now gone full circle and have actually moved their families back to Poland and they too commute to work. They have some serious pressures on them; they have young children as well, so they need to spend time with their families. So I told them several years ago, "Let's work out what you need to do to get the job done and to get your family life in sync." Their lives were a bit out of kilter and they were working too hard back then.

That might seem like a strange thing for a boss to say, but I knew it couldn't carry on like that for long. So we worked out a plan of working a certain amount of time as well as holiday time. Then I said, "Okay let's try and stick to that, but I'm not going to record anything and I'm not going to nickel and dime you. I'm not interested in exactly when you're on the building site or exactly what your time off is. I'm only interested in the job getting done. Make sure that that happens and I'll be the kindest, most generous boss that you've ever had." It works. They tell me when they're coming and going, but it's up to them to work out what balance they want and they know that they've got my full support.

I bought several of my builders cars over the years and had them pay me back from their wages. One of my builders wanted to buy an investment property from me once. I sat him down many times and told him about investment strategies: what he should be looking for, how he should be structuring deals, and then I lent him the deposit to buy the property. He bought three properties from us and he's now sitting on a net-worth of around half a million because of his very shrewd moves many years ago. I lent him all of the money to buy those properties and he paid me back. Those are some examples of us going beyond the traditional employer-employee relationship. It's been of benefit both to me and to my workers.

It now seems second nature for me to be an employer; it's who I am. I provide work for people. As well as providing for my family in Canada, I provide for 30 families in the UK as well. It's my responsibility to bring the work in for my staff. Now it's just part of my DNA. It's like a big family role almost. It's massively important to me — it's my second family over in Manchester.

And my workers feel the same way as well. They have consistently treated me way better than any boss deserves to be treated. They have gone beyond the call of duty and have worked tirelessly to produce one of the best businesses in the area. Whatever I have given to them has been paid back ten-fold with their hard work, loyalty and dedication. In fact, thinking about it, they were the ones who treated me the best to start with and I'm now trying to treat them well in return! Either way, it's a virtuous circle. I'm not sure exactly where it started, but it's one of the best feelings and it's business gold.

SECTION 5

PARTNERSHIP

Teamwork

Ironically, when I first met my wife, we didn't hit it off straight away. To be honest, we didn't give each other the time of day.

I met her a few months before I moved over to Whistler in a bar in London. A few years previously, she was a rep for an English holiday company in the French Alps. During that process she got a very bad impression of English skiers as being bad at skiing and a bunch of drunks, which probably isn't a million miles away from the truth when they're on holiday! My friend introduced us and said, "This is Pete, he's an English lawyer and he's going to go over to Whistler and do a season over there."

She sort of raised her eyebrows and said, "Okay." I thought she was a bit cold and frosty; I was quite happy to have a chat with her but I got a chilly response. So we didn't really talk to each other much that night.

The next time I met her, I was already in Whistler. I'd been there for a couple of years and now I could ski like a local. Both of us had feet in both the outdoor and the business worlds. I was very much an outdoor mountain person, but very much a businessperson, and felt quite at home in the city as well as the mountains. It's relatively rare that people bridge both worlds. You go in either one direction or the other I find.

Deborah, herself, had a foot in both camps so that was probably one of the main things that attracted me to her. The fact that I could go out and do a good day of skiing with her: she was adventurous, she was an outdoor girl. Yet she wasn't just leading her life depending on what the weather did, she was a hard-working professional as well. She's an award-winning interior designer and at the time was working with some of the biggest names in Vancouver real estate.

My first date with my wife took place on Valentine's Day in 2004. Funnily enough we went into a restaurant in Whistler, sat down, and they had put a couple of roses on the table and sprinkled sequin hearts everywhere. I leaned forward to Deb and said, "What's going on here? Have you told them this is our first date or something?"

She said, "No" and sort of looked at me.

"I don't understand. I didn't do this."

"You do know it's Valentine's Day, don't you?"

And I replied, "No. No I don't."

That's how focused I was on skiing and real estate at the time — I hadn't a clue what day it was!

Our partnership has been a big positive for my/our business. We started dating at the beginning of 2004. In the summer of 2006, we got engaged in Argentina in a mountain restaurant on a ski hill. Then we got married in 2007. When I met Deb, she was an absolute professional dealing with some very seasoned investors and developers in Vancouver; it made me realise what an amateur I was.

Deb is an award-winning designer. She won the IDIBC Award of Excellence, which is the Interior Designers Institute of British Columbia. In contrast, all of my early mentors were middle-aged white males typically from the North of England. They didn't put a great emphasis on interior design. It was more about churning out properties in a very bland, utilitarian manner: paint the walls magnolia, stick a tenant in there, put down the cheapest cord carpet you possibly could. In other words, you did the renovation for the cheapest price, making sure your costs were £500, and you rented it out for £600. That was their business plan (and it worked!), and that's one that I was doing at the time. Yet, I still (at that point) had half an eye on the fact that you could improve on the design side and make more money, so I tried to do a few amateurish design things myself.

Now Deb really rocketed that up. I must admit that when we first met, I thought that interior designers would spend a lot more money on a property than I wanted to and it was a type of money that I couldn't really work out where the return was going to be. Deb showed me that wasn't the case. Within two years of us meeting she'd left her job, she was working in the business with me and was designing our places to be some of the best apartments in the area. Every pound spent was getting between around £1.30 to £1.40 in return. So from me thinking that interior design was perhaps wasted money, it became clear that it was some of the best money I could spend. A good analogy is having a car. You can get a mechanic working on a car and doing all the stuff that you can't see in the engine. That's like the builders doing all the plumbing, the pipes, the electricity, the plastering. Yet, the stuff that you see — a nice coat of paint and the fixtures and fittings — is akin to polishing the car up just before you see it, rather than having a dirty car. It's not an expensive or large amount of money, it's a small percentage of the overall cost, yet it can be some of the best money you ever spend.

Deborah is fantastic at her job. She's far better at her job than I am at mine. I'm very privileged that we have an incredible designer working on 20-apartment schemes in Manchester, when she's qualified to be doing 400 to 500-apartment schemes in some of the best cities in the world. She works alongside raising our kids. What works best is for us both to have our separate roles. I just give her a flat budget for one particular show and let her spend that money on whatever she wants.

Deb really loves her job. I don't think that people who are in a standard profession (such as lawyers, doctors, accountants) can possibly like or love their jobs the way that she does. All the people that I work with who are fanatical about their jobs are creative types — either the architects or the interior designers — and are super passionate about what they do.

My wife is passionate about furniture, interior design, and buildings, so our holidays are always based around going somewhere that has smart architecture nearby. For our last holiday, we went to the Basque region San Sebastián, as they've got amazing architecture there. Deb constantly has her nose in a design magazine or book, of which we have hundreds in our house.

Having a husband and wife team is a big benefit for our business and our clients. It's like we're not two separate people. We're like one entity with two different sides. I'm always with my wife, so if you want to talk about the business, that's me and my wife. You don't need me to say "Oh hang on. I'm going have to talk to the interior designer about that or the architect," because if I've got Deb there she's answering that side of things. Me, I'm far more focused on the finance side of things. So we have some very good complementary skills between us.

Being married and having children has changed my life and my experience of running my business in so many positive ways. For a start, it gave me a very big, powerful "why." Before, my why was relatively selfish; it was all about me wanting to do things and improve my quality of life. Yes, I had a very big why in that I wanted to improve houses in a particular area and be the best in that one area. But my family adds a different dimension to that totally. Now my why is very much about my wife and children. I want to look after my family in a spectacular way. That's my role now, and that trumps everything else.

Sadie, my youngest, follows me everywhere and wants to be wherever I am. So I take her to the building sites and show her what's going on. It makes me proud to show my kids constructive work that's been done. Gabriel is very much a creative type; he's got his mum's thought process. He plans out buildings and villages, and he's very into art and drawing. I can see him becoming a budding architect.

We always talk about property because they know it's my job and their mum's job as well. If I cast my eye around the house, there's building plans everywhere: there's samples of materials, there's mortgage deeds, etc. The whole of the house is filled with things to do with real estate. Even if you look on our bookshelf, 90% of the books are about design or architecture or real estate investment. So, everywhere they go there is something to do with buildings.

Whenever we go to the UK, as we do every year for a big family trip, they're in and out of building sites the entire time. They hear me talking about work because I work from an office in my home. They are immersed in the building trade, the building game, the building industry. It's almost part of their DNA. We're building our family home over here in Canada as well; it's been a long process. So, they've seen the build going on, they hear me talking about it. They're being introduced to real estate at a very early age.

I would however never want my kids to go into my business unless they really wanted to. I've got no desire at all for Armistead and Son to be the family business in 30 years' time, or for it to become Armistead, Son and Daughter. If they wanted to out of their own free will, then great, but only if that's the way that they're inclined. I'd much rather they go out there and just choose their own path and follow their own dream, whatever that may be.

SECTION 6

SUCCESS PRINCIPLES

Kitchens sell properties!

Our design principles

So my wife has been a huge influence in creating the success of our business and in our design principles.

All of our interior design materials have been carefully chosen and the builders need to use the exact materials and colours they are given. If we're instructing our own in-house team, they know what to use, as they've got a set list of fixtures and fittings. If it's an external team, then we take them around our previous job sites, show them the standard that they're aiming for and give them a list of our fixtures and fittings, along with suppliers and cost. We never leave it up to the builders to make any design choices.

We have a high finish level and everyone knows the standards we're shooting for. I would never just pitch up on the last day and hope that a flat has been done. We've got the various professionals — builders, building regulations controller, structural engineer, architect and QS — all monitoring the work. We actually use the same key players the whole time, therefore, we have a fantastic team.

High standards for interior design

As I've mentioned, my wife is an award-winning interior designer in British Columbia. When she's designing an apartment she looks at everything as a holistic whole. She chooses the shade of kitchen to go with the types of tiles on the wall and the flooring. Everything is well-prepared, well-chosen and well-structured.

We have to get very good quality items at reasonable prices because most of the flats we're selling go for around about £250,000. Of course we do select nice things to stand out from the crowd: granite, quartz or marble kitchen counters. We do windowsills in the same material as well. We have oak flooring throughout as standard.

Our bathrooms usually have white tiles on the walls and a Victorian type of tile on the floor with modern chrome features: a power-shower and underfloor heating. Underfloor heating is eco-friendly; it's the best form of heating you're going to get. The Victorian tiles on the floor give a nod to the fact that most of our buildings are around 150 years old, but everything looks sharp. We've got to create a blank canvas so that anyone that walks in will like it. I'm not trying to bling the flats up, but at the same time they've got to really show a lot of quality, so most people who walk in will say, "Wow!"

Our properties have the same lighting throughout: all recessed pot lights. My wife does the lighting plan, and instead of just shoving in eight spotlights in a room like some developers, she will make sure that they're all exactly a certain amount of centimetres from the wall and pointing in the right direction to create the right mood and effect. They're directional rather than straight in your eyes when you walk in. We'll spend the same amount of money as another developer on our lighting, but we will do a far better job.

> **TOP TIP:** INVEST IN GOOD DESIGN AND ARCHITECTURE WHEN DEVELOPING PROPERTY. GOOD DESIGN SELLS!

For the garden, we want something smart and low maintenance. We also have full-time gardener as part of our team, with two guys going around and spending most of their summer gardening. Because we are doing blocks of 16 to 20 apartments, the garden space is often quite large. We think about who's buying these flats — they're usually young, affluent professionals — so they want somewhere nice to sit out, but don't want to do the gardening. They want nice plants around them, a spot of grass, a barbecue, a bench to sit down on and have a beer or glass of wine after work or on a Sunday afternoon. We design the gardens with the end user in mind.

Choosing the best tenants

As we have increased the quality of our accommodation over the years, we have been able to attract a better type of tenant. It has been my experience that in general, the more people are willing to pay for a property, the better they treat the property. Also, because they tend to work hard with longer hours, the wear and tear on the property is a lot less.

When we buy buildings that house tenants at the lower end of the spectrum, we sometimes have to evict tenants, and as you may imagine, we quite often have issues with that process. For a start, we're asking people to leave their homes, which isn't a great thing for neither us nor them. Quite often we've had people not paying any rent, just seeing how long they could get away with staying rent-free. Clearly, we've had to go through the court process.

We've had thousands of tenancies over the last 18 years or so, and we've had all sorts of tenants — from those who are rather strange to those who seem nice and normal. We had one situation where one young girl just disappeared. She left her flat with everything in there: mobile phone, wallet, all the things that you would really think that she would take with her, even if she just went down to the shop for a pint of milk. We tried to get in contact with her friends and the disappearance was eventually passed over to the police. We boxed all of her stuff up and that was that. We never saw her or heard anything about her again. That was a bit disturbing and strange.

We've probably had to go to court about ten times and evict tenants that were misbehaving in some way. A few years ago, someone was growing cannabis plants in one of the flats. It's hard to weed out every bad tenant — no pun intended! If we do get someone who is misbehaving, we have to come down quite hard on them because we have blocks of flats, so one tenant misbehaving could annoy the other 12 tenants in that block.

In general though, we have a very clear policy of providing some of the best accommodation and it tends to attract harder working tenants. So instead of having people that grow marijuana plants for a living, we tend to have doctors and lawyers.

The Nomad mindset

There has been a massive shift in mind-set since my days as a lawyer. I have embraced the nomad lifestyle of primarily working remotely. I realise that I'm not really mainstream any more. Even now, when people are used to remote working, I still don't fit into peoples' boxes. Someone will ask me, "What do you do for a job?"

I'll say, "Oh, I'm a real estate investor in Manchester."

They'll say, "So you're over here on holiday are you?"

"No, I live here in Whistler."

"Well, how does that work?"

Or, you're going through passport control at the airport and someone says to you, "Are you going home then?"

And you stumble and it's like, "I don't know. Maybe. I've got two homes really."

When you explain it to them, they get it, but it's not as natural as, "Yeah, I'm a lawyer. I live in London. I'm coming here to Canada because I've got a holiday home," type of approach. To work remotely can work very well, but you do need to do it properly. You need to be very self-reliant and quite disciplined.

SECTION 7

SURVIVING THE CREDIT CRUNCH

The credit crunch

The credit crunch didn't have an immediate impact on the property market. The sales and rental market, for the whole of 2007, was strong. If anything, it had signs of overheating. By the end of the year, however, it was clear that banks were in trouble and that there were many banks holding assets in the States. The idea back then was that this was solely an American problem as the American banks had been lending to the wrong type of people, but by early 2008 it was clear that the British banks were in trouble as well. At that time, the credit markets closed, banks stopped lending and we became aware that there was a full-blown banking crisis. It was as if someone had just stopped the music at the party. This wasn't just a bump in the road, it was a crash of epic proportions and it turned out that you could barely do business for a few years afterwards.

The effects on my business

Our business needed to keep moving and going forward to survive and thrive. If we just stood still and looked at our property portfolio, things balanced themselves out. Investing for cash flow was by far the least sexy side of the business. The reason I was in business was to buy, renovate and sell property, and it became almost impossible to do that. The fact that we had a good solid portfolio of properties generating good cash flow each month, was key to our resilience during the recession. We also did manage to do deals and build during this period, and in hindsight I'm proud that we managed to continue our building rate, albeit slowly. We were hobbling along but still continued to move forwards.

While we carried on building, the jobs we were doing were hard; they did not make much profit margin and the sales were very, very difficult. We had a couple of jobs which basically just paid the builders' salaries, without providing a profit margin. But the guys were family and had to be looked after.

At times, we were buying places and did not even know their resale value, but that was a way of keeping our builders at work. We had a couple of years where we found ourselves in an unprecedented situation and it became hard to forecast what would happen next.

This was not a normal recession — it was a real black swan event.

Because of my prior extensive lawyer-like research, I had business plans in place for dealing with normal recessions, but unfortunately, this wasn't one of those times. You got a sense that the world was about to end and the financial system worldwide could have just collapsed. I had friends that were talking about buying cheap islands in Canada, bringing their families with them, and escaping away from it all. Lots of people withdrew all of their money from the banks. Simply stated, it was a ridiculously bad time to be trying to do business. But we carried on regardless.

At the time, we were the only builders in our area who continued, and we struggled to do business. We had to come up with creative ideas since we couldn't borrow money from banks any more. We had to devise other business plans, work out different strategies. Our old strategy of buying with bank finance, renovating, selling or re-mortgaging was almost impossible. We had to deal with different lenders and come up with a different business plan fast.

There was lots of fear and inexperience coming from pretty much everyone when it came to dealing with this crisis, since nobody had lived through or experienced a recession like this before. During a classic recession, banks still carry on lending; you can usually access funds. It might be a little more expensive, interest rates may be a bit higher, costs will be a lot higher, but the banks keep lending. I'd read about these scenarios and knew what to do. But when the money supply is cut off, it poses a new question: how do you do business? I didn't want to be the guy that just sat on his hands; I wanted to carry on going forward doing business, making money and keeping my workers employed. That is a strong driving force for me: making sure that my family and my workers' families are ok.

I had read about contrarian investing. It's one thing reading the books and having the information in your head, but it's quite another to put it into action. It's an easy thing to read but a not-so-easy thing to actually do. It's easy to look at property prices and think, "Hang on, I can buy property 20% or 30% cheaper than a year ago." The thing is that you don't know how low that's going to go. You might be buying a pounds' worth of property today, and it might be worth 70p next year. That was the situation I was faced with during the recession. Everyone else around me stopped building and stopped doing business, but I made a conscious decision to carry on.

I certainly had my moments of self-doubt. There were also times when I was tempted to adjust my business plan and try something new. Back in 2008, if I told other investors that I was buying property and I was doing some of the biggest deals I've ever done, people looked at me and shook their heads as if to say, "You don't know what's going to happen. This is craziness. You are overpaying. Wait until next year: prices might be even cheaper."

That was the mentality of most people. Most investors didn't buy during the recession, though they should have. They didn't buy because they were either too fearful, or they wanted to see the green shoots of recovery first. But when you see the green shoots of recovery, it's too late. Things have already started moving, and you've missed your bargains. You do have to find the courage to jump in there. The time to be a contrarian investor and the best time to buy is at the darkest hour of a recession, and that's precisely what I did.

I am the kind of person who doesn't go half-heartedly into anything. If I pursue anything, I want to excel at it. I want to be an excellent real estate investor, I want to be an excellent skier, I want to be an excellent ultra-runner. I don't pick loads and loads of things that I want to be all right at. I'm not well rounded, but that's part of my personality.

When everything goes wrong, I'm not the guy who's going to crawl under a rock and just wait for it to pass by. My position during this period was more like, "Okay this is the biggest challenge in hundreds of years of real estate in the UK. You're actually quite lucky to be in this situation. You're not going to experience it again. No one else that you have been around has ever experienced this. This is it. It's the big tsunami. It's time to get stuck in and not just survive but to also thrive. You need to raise your game, come out fighting and be the best." It was a test of character as much as anything else.

Contrarian Investing

It was very much a case of having to go against the grain. I frequently asked myself, "Hold on a minute — am I doing the right thing here? Everyone else has stopped. Maybe I should stop, too?" We were in a situation where we could have just stopped. We had a good amount of equity, a nice amount of cash flow; we could've retreated for sure, but then we would have lost all competitive advantage. The market was going to turn. When? Nobody knew. I very much wanted to be last man standing, still building and improving during this period.

During this period, we didn't just carry on churning out the same bland old apartments; we got better. We needed to be the very best. We needed to be spectacular. I wanted people to walk into our apartments and say, "Wow! It's an amazing apartment. Even though the market's tricky, we are going to buy an Armistead Property apartment because it's so impressive. It's not just a normal property that's for sale. It's special." That was what we focused on: getting our build as good as we could. That gave us a massive competitive advantage.

Warren Buffett has a very famous quote, "Be fearful when others are greedy and greedy only when others are fearful." It was at that particular time that I recognised that. This was a time when fear was at its absolute height. This was therefore the time when the bargains were about. This was the time to be greedy and to try to do as much business as we possibly could. It was hard to do business, but I did some of my best business in the period between 2008 and 2010.

As none of the banks were lending, I realised that we had to either self-finance deals or hook up with other high net-worth individuals. There were many people around sitting on big pots of cash, which they'd gone from earning six per cent in the bank to earning zero per cent. They needed to do some deals and some business as well. Investing in real estate wasn't exactly what they wanted to do, but some of them recognised that there were deals to be done, and we ended up doing joint ventures that were profitable as a result.

I was a fanatical networker and during my networking I tried to meet as many high net worth clients as possible, although most of these investors were too scared to invest during this period. I did meet one particular investor who wasn't scared, though. This was Mike. He was an old-school landlord; he had many properties in our area — maybe 50 places — and we got into business together. He had the property, we had the skills, and he saw how amazing our apartments were. We discussed various business plans and one day I said to him, "Look I'm not borrowing money from the banks at the moment. I don't trust them and they're not lending anyway. How about you and me hook up in a partnership? You keep ownership of your properties. They are all quite old and tired, but with some intelligent development we can substantially increase their value and sell them. I will develop them to maximize their value and will share the profits. That way, I don't need to find the money to finance the property purchase. We'll produce the best properties in the area and we'll sell them." We did just that and it was one of the biggest and best transactions ever done in our particular area. It happened at the depths of the recession when many people were all running for the exit. We struck one of our biggest ever deals then and it worked out brilliantly.

Even to this day, I do joint ventures with that particular investor. We've developed a close relationship over the years and we both know and trust each other. We have always made excellent money together and he's happy to invest with us on pretty much any deal that we bring to him.

The banks

We were massively in debt to the RBS at the beginning of the recession years. They were everybody's bank of choice before the credit crunch and they would basically lend to anyone with a pulse. During the recession, they started calling all money back in. We had to work closely with our bank managers to ensure that process was done in a nice, orderly way. We devised a plan that enabled them to get their money, not as quickly as they wanted, but we worked out how it could be done. They realised that we were the best developers in the area and that we could provide them with money. We did what we said and paid them back. Other investors I know were not so lucky. It was different in Canada than it was in the UK during this period. People in Canada didn't know what I was talking about when I was talking about a recession. They had a six-month blip and then all was well. Their banks were the most conservative banks in the world before the recession, and then they were the most well financed banks during the recession; they just carried lending like there was no recession.

Nevertheless, in spite of this, I could not have borrowed money in Canada for British real estate (we did a buy a house in Canada during the recession and that was an easy process). Our business plan was to focus on what we were good at: the long-term business plan of building high-end apartments in South Manchester.

Creative finance

We did everything that we could think of to get money in from as many different sources as possible. We even wrote to all of our tenants in our properties and offered to sell them their apartments. I thought, "Look, if they're living there, they obviously like it. If we can offer them a bit of a deal, then we can sell them the property. It would be an easy decision for them and there would be money in it for us." So that was one strategy.

Focusing on finding investment other than from the banks became very important for us. I remember we took out quite a few bog-standard personal loans — just bank loans in our own personal names. We did that when we needed to finance either building work or the purchase of properties. We were looking after the pennies during this stage. There wasn't any unnecessary spending and we were very tight with the money that we spent during the recession.

I am sometimes asked: "How do you find high net worth investors?"

I think that they asked a famous bank robber once, "Why did you steal money from the banks?" and he replied, "Because that's where the money is!"

With high net-worth investors, you need to think where they are likely to be. Don't go down the local pub — unless you live in Chelsea — hoping to meet a millionaire investor. Instead, go to places where investors are likely to be. This means endless networking, endless seminars, endless conferences. If everyone's at a property conference, they're already convinced about real estate and probably know a bit about real estate already, so that's a good way in.

Think about how much money you want. If you're looking for £10,000 or £20,000, then many people have that type of money. You can ask your grandma or your auntie for example, and they might have that. If you want £1,000,000 then that's a different focus.

After you work out where rich people are hanging out, where investors are networking, any events that they're going to, then go to those places. If you find one guy who has some money and you're doing a deal, the chances are that he will know other guys with money — like attracts like. I've been lucky, and the harder I work, the luckier I get! I've met people who have invested with me and then passed other friends onto me.

I was flying business class a few years ago and I sat next to a person who had obviously paid a lot of money for his ticket, just like I had, and I was talking to him about real estate. He expressed an interest in it, so I carried on the conversation not expecting it to go anywhere (it was just a friendly chat). By the end of the plane journey, he had agreed to do a deal with me. A few months later, he bought a property from us and then he wanted to do a joint venture and had a substantial amount he wanted to invest. He's since introduced me to one of his other friends who has money to invest who wants to do a JV as well. It's all about constantly looking for the right type of people, and having a soft, inviting approach.

People say you should never mix business with pleasure but I feel the opposite way. I will 100% mix business and pleasure. The two things are the same for me. I know many people who will not do business with their friends just in case things go wrong. I am totally the opposite. If I have a good deal and everyone is going to make money out of it (I have never lost money for anyone), I am happy to share it and I'd rather my friends benefit. I've done several hundred transactions and they're always profitable. I'd rather one of my friends or one of my contacts make a good amount of money than some acquaintance I've only just met.

Always mix business and pleasure. It is pleasurable doing business; it's not a hard slog for me at all. The work is fantastic, and I'd rather do business with friends and people I like. I'll only do business with someone I don't like or someone I don't respect if it's just a one-off property transaction. If you don't like and respect the person, it won't be a long-lasting, good, solid relationship.

Rallying the troops

My staff were reading the papers and coming in to work worried about their jobs during the credit crunch years. Everyone was on red-alert; it was obvious what was going on. I put a positive spin on it. I told them, "Look, everyone else has stopped doing business. We are going to go forward doing business. Things are going to change inevitably. Our business plan is going to change and our funding method is going to change, but that is a problem for *me* and that's on *my* shoulders. That's my name on the door and the buck stops with me. What I need from you guys is your best work going forward, because that's our business plan. We are going to produce the best flats in the area and that's how we sell them when other people are not selling their properties."

They had their problems to worry about, like when the scaffolding was coming or how the drainage system was going to work, or how many millimetres of insulation we were going to put in a basement. But the idea was: "We will carry on going forward and we will put a smile on our faces because we are the only guys selling flats during the recession. We're in a great position and in a year or two, we will have firmly cemented ourselves as the best in the area. People will be coming in asking for one of our properties."

During the recession, we never had to let anyone go. I wanted to keep our core team of workers and that's exactly what I did. Our workers then cemented themselves as the best workers in the area. We produced the best flats. We are the number one developer now.

For us, the tough times were from 2008 to 2012. Even though we did some good business then, they were still tough times. By 2012, we had paid back all of our debts to the banks. That felt like the shackles being lifted!

How did I do it? How did I motivate my troops during those difficult four years? With lots of encouragement, pizza and beer! We used to have what I called building site parties, where we would pitch up on a Friday night to whatever building site we were on and we'd sit down, have a few beers and the pizza delivery boy would come and we'd have a few slices of pizza. It was a delightful couple of hours' worth of laughter and socialising, and we did that pretty much every month. We still do regular Friday night drinks, a meal out, things like that — every Christmas we have a big meal out in Manchester city centre. It's important for morale, and it's also really good fun.

Dealing with stress

Dealing with stress is a topic that was particularly relevant during the credit crunch years. I am happiest when I'm working hard and my mind is racing. I like being busy and getting things done. I move fast and I like causing a bit of havoc every now and again.

It's funny as my wife is the opposite. My wife is into yoga; she's a qualified yoga teacher, she meditates and has calm in her life. I don't have calm in my life like she does.

The only time I am calm is when I'm exercising, skiing or ultra-running, and I get myself into that type of state. I don't actively go out to get myself into a state of calm and the most important thing for me is working hard and covering as many options as I possibly can for success and failure in my mind.

SECTION 8

THE GREEN SHOOTS OF RECOVERY

Glimmers of hope

In 2012, when we had paid the banks off, I saw the first green shoots of recovery where I thought, "Okay, things are starting to look up" and I started to feel a bit more optimistic about the economy. We were able to work for ourselves again and we weren't being hamstrung by the banks. We could get away from that and do proper business again. All of this marked a key turning point for us.

The market was recovering; other banks were starting to come back into the market. It was the best part of four years that the banks were effectively closed for business. But new "challenger" banks came through sensing a gap in the market, banks that weren't saddled with all the old debt that the traditional banks were. So we were able to start doing a bit more business.

People were sick to death of the recession and they were buying properties more from 2012 onwards. It wasn't a big upward trajectory — it was a bumpy road, but it was a road we were fine being on. It was better than the previous four years.

The business environment definitely improved from 2012 onwards and Manchester especially has a very progressive council that is focused on granting planning permission and encouraging professionals to come to the city. The recovery in Manchester has been a lot better than the national recovery and it's been an exhilarating and vibrant place to do business.

Boxing clever

I did not intentionally set myself a goal to expand and take on larger and larger developments. It happened organically. I did not have this goal during the recession because it was almost impossible to do financial planning from 2008 to 2012. The key skill during that period was to box clever: to stand there in the middle of the ring and say, "Whatever comes at me, I can handle." We've still pretty much got that mind-set.

I set goals, but in more of a general way than I used to. There's definitely no "buy 50 properties in 50 months" goal any more. There are goals of where I want to get to: the size of developments, the type of developments, the type of team I want. But things are a lot more flexible now with my goal setting.

The business environment today is at quite a strong level and similar to before the credit crunch and I could probably define more precise financial goals for myself and the business. Looking at the returns I'm making at the moment, how we're doing business, I still like the goal of being the best in the area, which perhaps sounds a little bit woolly, but it means a lot to me. Plus, growing organically. They're the two things that we've been focusing on.

Investing in Manchester today

We still primarily invest in Chorlton and Whalley Range/Old Trafford today. Chorlton prices and rents are 20% above Whalley Range prices, therefore you can spend a little bit of extra money on a Chorlton job. So absolutely every single flat we do in Chorlton has a £2,000 granite work surface in the kitchen. Sometimes we have to think carefully about this decision if it's a Whalley Range or Old Trafford flat. Sometimes it's worth it, sometimes it's not. It's a similar set of patterns, but we have an A and a B plan and we can switch between them needed. We can just tone things down from the absolute Rolls Royce job, if necessary.

I love old buildings. They're the best. Part of it is economics — it's supply and demand. My clientele are 30-year-old millennials and they all aspire to live in Victorian properties that are cool and cutting edge internally. Overall, they would rather live in a timeless classic like that than in a new-build.

New-builds look great for the first five or ten years of their life and then they start to look dated. Whereas somewhere that was done 150 years ago has already become a timeless classic with widespread appeal. I've never had someone come and say, "I don't like old buildings. I just want a modern one." It almost never happens. I look at supply and demand and that's where the demand is.

To give you an idea of the type of developments that we do: we might buy a block of 16 apartments in a big, old Victorian mansion. The bigger the better. Then we do them up with modern interiors. We will take a tatty old building, ideally the ugliest building on the street. We will develop and make it look gorgeous from the outside. Chances are we often do something modern at the back – perhaps stick on an extension that has quite big windows and lots of glass letting the light in. We create large open plan-style apartments that are very modern internally.

Everyone loves living in old Victorian buildings, but they don't want draughty old sash windows and damp walls. People want something smart and efficient. We put the two aspects together: our properties are smart and high-end internally — lovely and well-repaired — yet they are still 150-year-old buildings externally.

I personally get a real sense of history and achievement with turning these old, knackered buildings into something beautiful. That gives me a fantastic sense of pride and satisfaction. I doubt I would get that if we just purely did new-builds and everything was boxy and modern design. Renovating old properties is a far more interesting business plan for me. The downside is that it is harder to scale it. If you wanted to do 400 apartments, it is a lot easier to do that in one great big new-build than it is to do spread over 20 older properties.

The history of the properties we develop is also part of the attraction. I have a local historian who researches all of our buildings for us. This is something which most property developers don't do but its proved very useful and very interesting for me. He's a retired history teacher, Andrew Simpson, a local legend in Chorlton. It's mainly for my own personal interest and enjoyment but I've learnt a lot of stuff from him about our local area. For example, he was able to tell me where the underground rivers were. It's also been good background work for every single deal that I've done.

It gives me a great sense of satisfaction to know a little more about a building's past. For example, our latest development at Carlton Terrace where we have 16 apartments was originally a merchant's house, then became a doctor's surgery during World War I. Manchester has been there since the Roman times, so it has a lot of history.

The local historian has found out quite a few quirky things about properties that we have developed or worked on. One building that we bought was the headquarters for local gangsters many, many, years ago; it was a criminal enterprise! We've bought many residential homes. One home we bought belonged to an MP. We've also just bought a school. Most of the properties we buy are residential houses, so it's a case of tracking the inhabitants of them as well and finding out what they did. If you have a house that has been there for 150 years, there's usually a good amount of interesting history attached to it.

We found one house where there was a hidden room once. It was in the basement, it was built next to an external wall, and it had all been blocked off. There was no way you could have seen this room until we stripped everything back to brick. There was just a small hidden room there. We do not know what its purpose was, but it was strong and secure. It was maybe for illegal activity or for keeping something down there that someone didn't want anyone to find. It was almost like a bank vault when we went in there; it was a strange thing to find.

Another building we bought had DJ equipment in it: tens of thousands of pounds worth of music equipment in the basement. We didn't know exactly what it was until we started researching it and sold it on. People leave all sorts of strange things about, but it's normally the unwanted stuff; it's rare that you find anything decent. We get lots of old, knackered bikes and used baby gear that's better off in the skip!

The worst buildings

Of course, I couldn't write a book about property investing without telling you about some of the challenges we've had and some of the worst buildings that we've done up.

I bought a crack house once, for example. They were two blocks, side by side, with 11 units in there. I went around and couldn't even get into some of the apartments. There were squatters living in the apartments that should have been empty. In one of the flats there was a dead dog. It was pretty grim and disgusting.

Even when we had cleared all the tenants out, they used to break back in in the evening and they would be using it as a brothel and a crack-dealing site. We had to secure it and get some additional physical security to monitor the site for us. That was bleak. We saw people in the worst states, at the very bottom of their game. There were some sad individuals that I met during that time.

I was aware of the issues when I bought the property but it was still quite daunting. We bought it at an incredible price and I was expecting all the problems to go hand in hand with that. I'd been around to see it and I'd worked out quite quickly what was going on. I knew what we were letting ourselves in for. That's one where we did have to get our hands dirty to evict the tenants and to secure the building.

The process probably took about four months to get everybody out properly because people kept breaking back in. We had to get it off their radar. Most druggies have a short-term outlook on life. It tends to be, "Where can I get my next rock from?" and that's pretty much it. I have five-year and ten-year business plans. Some Japanese companies have 100-year business plans. Druggies seem to have a business plan that's the next hour or two and that's the wavelength that they're on. When it became clear that this was not a place they could go and buy crack, use crack, use prostitutes — that it was a building site — they found another building. We just had to get it off their radar.

A business 8,000 miles away

All property investors look for more deals and more money to buy the deals. As we started to recover from the recession, it made sense for me to find a full-time property sourcer to find deals, so that I could focus a lot more on working on the business, not in it. I focus more on both bringing in bank finance and creative finance from private individuals as well. If you can focus on both those two elements, that's the business growing in a good, exponential way.

I've set up a business that is actually quite traditional in the way it's run, even though I manage it remotely. It's a real estate business at the end of the day. This is not a big tech industry. The tech changes that have happened in real estate are minor compared to many other industries in the last 10 or 20 years. We have an operational and reporting structure and hierarchy that is similar to many businesses that you would see in the UK.

We have a property management side with a reporting structure where every single property is itemised. It's split into sections — rents, maintenance, other issues — and each week when the head of the rental business compiles the report and sends it to me, he puts in any changes, any maintenance that's happened with a particular property, any tenants that aren't paying their rents on time; just as a normal business would. The difference is that instead of everyone coming in and putting it on my desk, they e-mail it to me. I'm not sitting next door to them in a separate office; I'm 8,000 miles away in my office in Canada in a different time zone. I get the same report. It's just that our business structure is streamlined so that it can run remotely.

I admire Tim Ferris and his book *The Four Hour Work Week*. He's an inspirational, charismatic guy and the way he advises working is very similar to the way I manage my work. He's not just some big, fat CEO that's earning millions and smoking cigars. Tim Ferris is a man of the future: he's in great physical shape, he's charismatic, he's a speaker, and he's a businessman. You're never going to see him in an old-school pin-stripe suit following the crowd and leading an uneventful life.

I don't necessarily take on board his concept of the four-hour work week – I admire and look forward to hard work. Building your brand and getting your business up to a good state takes time. I've not focused on a goal of only wanting to work four hours a week — I don't. I want to work four hours in the morning, and then when the morning is over, I can do another four hours in the afternoon, and another four in the evening — and do that six times a week!

I'm not on the wavelength of working for only four hours. But I am definitely on the same wavelength of running my business from cool, exotic locations. In my time over the last 18 years, I've run my business from over 30 different countries including places like: Hawaii, Majorca, Australia, Bali, Greece, Argentina, New Zealand, Alaska, Canada, Spain, Portugal and France. There have been many places where I've just set up shop for a month or so, and run the business from there, and it's worked well. It doesn't matter where I am. That's what I want. I'm happy to work hard, but I want to be able to do this anywhere in the world. That's the structure that I've set up for my business. That's why we have the staff, the operational structure and reporting structure that we have. This is what my business is all about.

If I can do anything digitally, I prefer to. We have a bog standard traditional office in Manchester. We have filing cabinets full of paper there, but a lot of our information is all uploaded to the cloud and is shared and accessed remotely.

If it were not for the Internet and computers, I'd be struggling. It's the advent of technology that has allowed me to have this freedom. When I set off on my journey 18 years ago, it was doable in theory but very few people were actually pursuing a successful business nomad lifestyle. Now, it is far more common, especially in North America. Things are more advanced there with regards to technology. My business is primarily operating remotely in the Cloud.

Partnering and JVs

I've touched on this before earlier in the book, but it's so important it's worth going over again. Choosing the right JV partners is crucial to the success of a business deal.

When I'm meeting someone at a networking event, I have a kind of your mental checklist of, "Is this person a good fit for me?"

What they want, how much money they have to invest is key. If I'm looking at my next project, which is several million, it's not worth my time talking to someone that's just got £10,000 and has never invested in real estate at all. I'd rather be looking at someone who knows what they are doing, is a sophisticated investor, has a good amount of money, and has done deals before. Many people say they will do things and they never do. It is important to me that I get a feel that someone will commit when they say they will.

That's often a gut feeling, but if you're wanting someone to make an investment it's better if they know and understand the process of making investments in the first place. If it's someone you have to educate about real estate and doing investments, chances are they are not the type of people that you want to be dealing with anyway.

I'm often asked what my tips are for approaching someone and broaching the subject of finance or a JV. In other words, is it best to start chatting socially first or better to go straight in there and say that you invest in real estate and are looking for money?

With me, I never make the first move. I will always talk about things that I like and that I know about. It might be nattering away about current affairs, the weather, skiing, living in Canada. I have various topics of conversation that I know people think are quite amusing. If I find out someone exercises, I'll ask if they. If the answer is yes, I'll tell them I'm an ultra-runner.

They'll say, "What does that mean exactly?"

"It means last weekend I ran a 122-mile race over 33 hours without stopping." I know that's going to guarantee an interesting conversation. Or, I'll ask them about something interesting that they might have done recently. I never throw business in there straight away. You don't want to come from a position of desperation or make them feel defensive.

When they work out you're a real estate investor and you sell high-end, boutique investments, if they're interested, they'll raise it. They'll say something like, "Okay, do you do good deals with people then?" or they'll ask, "Is there a discount if I buy from you?"

To which you can laugh and say, "There's always a deal to be done." Then you're down that route. You should almost never approach someone and say, "Here we go, I'm looking for £100,000 for a couple of years worth of investment."

Those approaches don't work. I always find that the soft approach is better. Take people out for cups of coffee. Show them your developments. If you're doing some great work and you're proud of it take them around and show them. Just say, "Look, this is what we're doing right now." Then, if people appear interested, and you've spent a bit of time with them, you can go down the investment route. You need to build up the relationship and put the foundations in before you should even start talking about a deal. Let them put it forward first. If they don't, then you're going to have to spend more time putting in the ground work before you're at the stage to say, "I know you like our stuff. If you're interested, there is an opportunity. We're raising finance now at 15% return per annum. I just thought I'd let you know."

Go business class

Here's another good tip for you if you're thinking of becoming a property nomad yourself and the lifestyle appeals to you. As soon as you can afford it, travel Business Class because: a) you get a bed and a couple of glasses of champagne, which is always nice — it makes it a pleasure rather than a chore, and b) business class is full of wealthy people. I have done multi-million pound deals purely through buying a business class ticket and sitting next to the right people. I look forward to my travelling days now — they're great experiences.

Here's another small helpful tip to ensure you're nice and relaxed before the flight. I have a President's Club Card for the Fairmont chain of hotels and they have lots of airport hotels. The card is free to get; you don't even need to have stayed in their hotels. They just give you the card; you can go online and get one now and it gives you free access to all the gyms and saunas in any of their hotels around the world, and they have a lot of airport hotels. I take my gym gear with me when I travel and I know, for example, at Vancouver airport I will go and check in, make sure I'm on time, and then I'll go and use the gym. I'll work out for an hour and get myself fit and healthy, all loosened up, have myself a nice sauna, an apple, a bit of mineral water and that sets me up well for sitting down for the next 16 hours or so. That's one specific tip to make your journey more pleasant.

SECTION 9

LIVING THE DREAM

Making good use of space. If the ceilings are high, we often add a mezzanine bed deck

Ultra-running

The skiing took a bit of a dip down following my completion of the 50:50 challenge, the birth of my first child, and — sadly — the deaths of a few close friends from skiing accidents. They were as good as you get as skiers, and they just made simple mistakes. One skied over the wrong piece of snow and fell down a crevasse; another skied the wrong shoot and it avalanched and sent him over a cliff. Three friends died within a few months, all young, and that rather shook me up a bit. After that, things definitely toned down a level and I didn't want to go skiing off 40-foot cliffs any more. I still ski every single day I can when I'm in Whistler, but I stopped searching out the craziest slopes on earth several years ago.

Around this time about five years ago I did my first mountain running race. I came fifth overall. It was only a 10k course up a few mountains and around a few lakes but I was instantly hooked. I instantly started reading more about mountain running and soon discovered that the ultimate bad-ass runners were out there running 100-mile races.

In an ultra-marathon (any race over 26.2 miles long), you need to be responsible for yourself and take all of your gear with you — you're running for up to 40 hours, navigating the wilderness and the mountains. At the time, that just seemed crazy to me. How on earth could a person do that? I decided to find out!

I chose ultra-running, or rather it chose me, for some strange reasons. It's a very mountain focused sport. We almost never run on roads, it's all dirt trails through trees and alpine passes. You don't need to be a particularly fast runner. It's more a war of attrition. But you do need to be responsible for yourself and get yourself through whatever conditions are out there. Whereas normal marathon running is usually done on a flat road, the terrain and conditions vary immensely from race to race in an Ultra, and as you are out there for

30-40 hours rather than maybe 3 for a marathon, you really need to deal with whatever is thrown at you. That's actually where I feel that I have a competitive advantage. It's about boxing clever and being very prepared — exactly what dominates my personal and business life.

Now I have both a winter and a summer obsession! I ski in the winters and mountain run in the summers. And I always work on my business!

I now go off running for long training runs – four to five hours is a normal, common, long training run for me. I wouldn't be able to do that often as a lawyer!

It's quite common for me to go for most of my long training run and not see people. One time, I'd been running for quite a while, and not seen anyone, when all of a sudden I heard a big scramble through the trees. I looked around and a cougar (a 200lb carnivorous mountain lion) was running through the trees directly at me. It jumped down on the trail and challenged me. It got within about 10ft of me and was staring straight at me. It was massive. It would've been able to kill me very easily. There's no two ways about that.

But, I did exactly the right thing in that situation. Bizarrely, I was not scared. Instinct kicked in. I shouted and screamed at it, raised my hands in the air, and made myself look big and menacing, which is quite hard considering that I'm 5'5", 135lbs, and generally quite a smiley, jokey guy. But I stood my ground and challenged it.

Wild animals don't want to take an injury so if they're not 100% certain of being able to get a kill they'll get out of there. That's what happened. It wasn't used to humans, it didn't know what it was getting involved with, so it disappeared and went looking for easier prey. I obviously cut my training run short. After the actual event then endorphins and all the emotions kicked in. I got out of there as quickly as I could and got in touch with the conservation officers.

Strangely, I felt no fear while this was actually taking place. I realised I was in a fight situation instantly. I knew this was very serious and that I had to be on my top game, and if I was going to go down I'd be going down fighting. I was working out exactly what I had to do to come out on top in that situation. I was thinking about weapons and what I had to hand to deal with this situation. Quite often, I have bear spray or a knife on me, but I didn't on this particular occasion. All I had was a bottle of water and some food. I can remember thinking within a split second, "What a silly time not to have a knife with me. What am I going to do: throw a bottle of water at it?" I quickly glanced about on the floor to see if there was a big stick lying about or any stones. But, I can remember thinking that even if there was, I didn't want to bend down and get the stick or the stone because then I'd be making myself small and looking as though I was retreating.

A lot of thoughts were flashing through my mind and this was all happening within a split second. It was fast, and my thought processes were racing. Everything was very clear though, there was no fear or panic whatsoever. None. If anything I was already in a relatively fuelled up, highly emotional state anyway, because I was running in nature, and I quite often lose myself in the experience. I remember even thinking that if it came towards me I was going to charge at it at the same time because it wouldn't expect me to attack.

The cougar quickly turned, did a 180-degree spin, and ran away through the trees. It didn't want a fight with me. If I'd have turned and ran, then it would've been a very different situation. It would've chased me down and killed me. There are some good business analogies in that episode!

When I go running these days, I always know that there is the potential to bump into wild animals – bobcats and bears or lynx –

when I'm out and about and at times I do feel quite vulnerable. There are many places that I go running. One is about 20 miles down the road from me and it's a very good place to go running. It's lower down and out of the mountains somewhat and as it doesn't snow as much down there I can run there pretty much all year round. However there's lots of cougars there and I always take protective gear with me — a knife and bear spray — if I'm running there. In Whistler, there is not so much of a cougar problem and so I feel a little safer in the mountains. Although in reality, the threat is always there; there are always cougars around and you need to be careful (again, another business analogy!). That's why I hadn't bothered taking a knife or bear spray, when I encountered the cougar. I thought it was a bit of overkill.

Now, if I'm doing my long runs solo, and I know that I'm going off where I could be many hours away from civilisation, I quite often take the next door neighbour's dog with me. It's a young male Doberman and is a very loyal dog. As long as I've got a bit of company, it's always nice. As in business, it's good to sometimes have a partner with better skills in certain areas then you have.

Award for Excellence: The UK Property Awards Best Renovation

The culmination of all the years of hard work came with winning The UK Property Awards Best Renovation for 2017-2018.

The UK Property Awards are prestigious; they're the premier award that you can get. We entered last year for one of our jobs which was a Rolls Royce job; we'd done an amazing amount of work on it. It was a two-year build project for us. The quality was sky-high, just through the roof. We entered the award and we won it.

That was a massive pat on the back for all of us and it's the end result of 18 years of focusing on quality and high build standards. There's been a big emphasis in our business of building the best designed and the best built flats. We keep many the properties that we build and they rent amazingly well and there are almost no maintenance problems. It's worth buying one of our properties from us just because you're not going to maintain it at all for the next ten years or so. It's not going to need a stitch of work done to it.

So to get that award meant so much to me and the team. It was the culmination of great team work and a fantastic pat on the back for my staff.

The emotional journey

None of this would have been accomplished had I not had massive shifts in my mind-set from being an employed lawyer to being an investor and then to being a business owner. Being an investor and a business owner are two very different things.

It was a massive shift. It's always a work in progress and is still going on today in a way as deep down, I am still a lawyer and I'll always be a lawyer. Once you've had that training inside you, it's always there. I've got lawyer skills. I worked hard for them and I use them daily.

The general principles that I learned about analysing in detail are great, but quite often if you analyse too much, you're wasting time. The analytical skills I learned as a lawyer don't enable you to make decisions and do deals quickly enough in the real fast-moving world of real estate. You need to make the analysis a bit more flexible and a less rigid than you would if you were a lawyer. Operating on an 80 per cent knowledge base is fine in the real world. You don't have to sit there in your basement, grinding away researching and researching and researching until you get what you think is 100 per cent certainty, because if you do that, someone else has already got the deal. In any event, when you buy a property and start working on it, you inevitably encounter surprises and changes you couldn't possibly have foreseen.

When I was a lawyer, I was an employee. Yes, I was working long hours, but at the end of the day, I had very good job security. No one was going to sack me. I would go to work every day, work hard, get it all done and get a decent salary. As soon as you step away from that, it is really a case of "you eat what you kill," so it's up to you to go out there. If you want to be lazy for a couple of months and just go and sit on a beach somewhere you can do that, but chances are you're not doing any business. You're not making any money while that happens. It's up to you; you need to be as proactive, and as good as you can possibly can be, and that takes a lot of drive. Now, if you have structured your business correctly and have your phone and laptop with you, then the beach is a fine place to do business from.

Living on Easy Street

Living the dream wouldn't be the same without creating a dream home for myself and my family. I mentioned earlier in the book that my wife and I are currently building our dream own home in Whistler. I'm very proud of this so I've saved the best until last!

Easy Street, Whistler, is where our family home is that we're building. Yes, that's right: we will soon be living officially on Easy Street. It's my favourite residential street in Whistler because of the name and because it is right next door to the school, tucked away in a quiet little area. The school is separated by a small forest and our house is there at the edge of the forest. So, when we send the kids to this school, they will be jumping the fence in the morning and walking through the forest to school each day. It's perfect. You couldn't write it down any better. It's going to be amazing.

My wife and I had this plan of building our own dream home in Whistler for a while. We found a site a couple of years ago; it had a house on it, but the house was grotty and ripe for knocking down. So we bought the house with plans to build our dream home on the plot.

Then my wife, in true fashion, was driving past one particular house one day and she said, "Stop the car! Stop the car! Isn't that house amazing?"

I looked at it and I said, "Yeah it's okay."

And she said, "No, that's the house. I need to find out who that architect is. I need that architect to design *our* house. How do I do that, Pete? You're the real estate expert." With all my years of hard work and real estate knowledge I said, "Erm... You knock on the door and ask the owners!"

So, we did. My wife knocked on the door and said, "Excuse me, who designed your house for you?" And in a fashion that I have come to expect of my wife, she happened to pick the best and probably most expensive architect in the whole of British Columbia. He'd been on the front cover of *Dwell Magazine* and had received numerous awards. He was an absolute rock star and she managed to pick the one house he'd designed out here in Whistler. So, we instructed him and my wife and he started designing our dream home.

In design terms, his buildings are pretty much "modern boxes": boxes with a twist. Everything is 90 degrees or straight lines. You're not going to get a sloped roof on one of his properties. His roofs are all flat. We instructed him a couple of years ago and the job is almost finished now.

The walls are white, the floor is a polished grey concrete, all the bathroom tiles are white, the fixtures and fittings are all white, even the quartz counter top is white. Everything is good quality, carefully designed, but relatively neutral. My wife likes to get her colour and her excitement out of the furniture, so we'll have brighter cushions or smart designer coffee tables. Then those can be changed as and when we need to.

I'm not just excited about this personally as a home, but also from a developer's point of view it's been an amazing project to be involved with.

It's boxy with a flat roof, huge big deck, and floor-to-ceiling windows at the front and back. We've built up the front of the house where there's going to be a grassy lawn. It's an upside down house with the kitchen and living area upstairs. We've got mountain views, with a massive deck when you open the windows. We've got beautiful views, but we wanted the kids to be able to run about where we could see them. How do you do that if you've got your living and kitchen area upstairs? You have to build the garden up, so that's what we did. We lifted the garden up by building this great big mound of earth so that we can open the patio doors, the kids can run about and play and go down the road and back up again and we can keep an eye on them. There's a triple garage that's buried underneath the garden. We've got two big rooms that we're going to use as offices in the house as well. It is mega. It's going to be an amazing place for me to work from. It's going to be a smart, cool, modern house and that's my wife's dream — she loves modern buildings. I didn't even know it was my dream, but it is.

Island getaway

At the same time as creating our dream home, we've also bought ourselves a little bit of paradise. "The islands" are a group of islands between Vancouver and Vancouver Island. There are lots of tiny little islands around there. It's hippy heaven. Lots of Americans went over there to escape the Vietnam draft and the result is very artistic, creative, hippy-like communities.

My wife, Deborah, has grown up in Vancouver and it's quite the dream to live in Vancouver, have a winter place in Whistler, and to have a summer place on the islands. That's what everyone aspires to. They don't aspire to own a Ferrari or that type of thing — it's more about getting the best out of life, experiences and where you live.

Deborah has always wanted a place on the islands. Gambier is one of the closest islands. As soon as this place came on the market a few months ago, Deborah instantly phoned me up. She said, "It's perfect. It's a three-bedroom cabin, off the grid, in a sunny location right by the beach. It's got its own private dock that goes down into the water." We have to generate our own power supply through solar panels since there isn't any electricity. So, it's like camping in a three-bedroom wooden cabin that resembles something that the English would call a garden shed.

So, we bought it and that's our little island retreat now. Richard Branson's got Necker Island; we've got our own tiny little spot on Gambier Island. Two very different places, but the principle is the same!

The future

I would never have thought while I was growing up, and focusing on being a lawyer, that this is where I'd end up. My childhood was spent growing up in a quite deprived area of Manchester in a very loving family with a great, big emphasis on hard work and academics. My whole childhood was spent trying to work hard enough academically to get myself out of East Manchester and to London to be a lawyer. I wanted to be as lawyer ever since I could remember. Wearing a smart suit, driving a nice car and working in London — that was everything to me right the way through the whole of secondary school, university and after. I simply wanted to be a city guy driving a nice car and wearing a nice suit.

Pretty much as soon as I got there, I realised that that sort of lifestyle wasn't all it was cracked up to be and certainly wasn't what I wanted. I wanted more. I wasn't a massively outdoor kid when I was younger, certainly not to the extent that I am now. Although, all of my happiest memories when I was a kid were doing something outdoors such as camping holidays in the Lake District and places like that. We used to go away camping a lot and I loved it.

In one sense, I've already achieved my major goals. The quality of life that I have set up for myself can get no better. It's my idea of living the dream and I've been doing this for the last 18 years. There's nothing better that I would want to do or be. If someone said, "You can have a lifestyle swap with anyone in the world, pick anyone." Not a chance.

The goals I had 20 years ago have been achieved. Now, it's a case of achieving more and doing better at the things that I've chosen. So yes, I want my business to be bigger and better, I want it to carry on evolving and growing. And yes, I want to achieve more with my lifestyle choices.

Some people might say: "Well why don't you stop? You've achieved all of the things you've wanted to achieve; why don't you just set by a swimming pool and drink cocktails?" If I wanted that to be my goal it could be. But it would not be me. If someone said, "Would you rather sit by a swimming pool or do eight hours' worth of work?" I'll do the eight hours' worth of work, or I'd rather do a run for 33 hours.

I'm doing exactly what I want; I'm not being forced to do it and I'm not fitting into someone else's preconceived idea of how they think I should behave. My goal is to work hard and carry on running my successful business. My goal is to go skiing and ultra running. My goal is to have a cabin on an island off the coast of Canada which is off the grid. My goal is to have a cool, architecturally designed award-winning home in Whistler. So, I'm doing what I want. Right now I'm not making sacrifices or compromises. In the past, I did have times where I was not leading the lifestyle I wanted and I was okay doing that because it was part of a plan to enable me to achieve the goal. Sometimes you need to delay the gratification, but I'm not going to wait until the standard retirement age to start enjoying life.

In one sense, I will never retire because I love working too much and I will always be investing, even if I am no longer able to run a business as successfully as I would like. In another sense, I have already retired as I have the total freedom to do whatever I want, whenever I want. I am financially free and I have the freedom of time and choice, that usually only comes with retirement.

Right now, I am living the dream every day. It's been a long journey, but an amazingly enjoyable one. Your dream lifestyle is available, if you want it. You need to plan. Failing to plan is planning to fail. Hopefully, the principles in this book will give you some guidance and enable you to choose and live your own dream lifestyle.

CASE STUDIES

53/55 ZETLAND RD, MANCHESTER

A development of 8 boutique apartments in a prominent location in Chorlton, designed by award-winning architect, Simon James. Contemporary apartments set in a pair of Victorian Semis. This was a build-to-sell project.

We took two old semi-detached houses which were in a bad state of repair and converted them into eight apartments. We extended the property and put in a roof dormer, as well as digging down into the cellars to create a lot more amazing livable space. This was a 14-month project. The first phase of six flats sold out in one morning when released.

CARLTON TERRACE, OLD TRAFFORD

Development of 16 apartments in a mansion house-style property. High-end accommodation focused on the young, affluent, professional market. This development featured some of the highest specifications we have done to date and we successfully raised the ceiling price for apartments in the M16 postcode.

Winner of the prestigious UK Property Awards Renovation Prize, 2017.

This was a big job. The original building was an old doctors' surgery that had been badly converted into several bedsit-type units. This was one of the worst properties in the area and really wasn't fit to be lived in. We applied for planning permission for 16 large 2 and 3 bed units and, after a period of negotiation with Trafford Council, we were successful. The build was 15,000 sq. ft. and took us nearly 16 months to complete. We used high-end finishes and the flats have been recognised as the best in the area.

DENBIGH VILLAS, Manchester

This is one of our current developments. Originally a school, we obtained planning permission for 12 high-end apartments with a roof-top terrace. This development will commence in the summer of 2018, and will be the best development done in the desirable Chorlton area of Manchester. We are looking to create new standards of apartment living and also to raise the ceiling price of apartments in this area. This will be a build-to-sell project.

THE AUTHOR

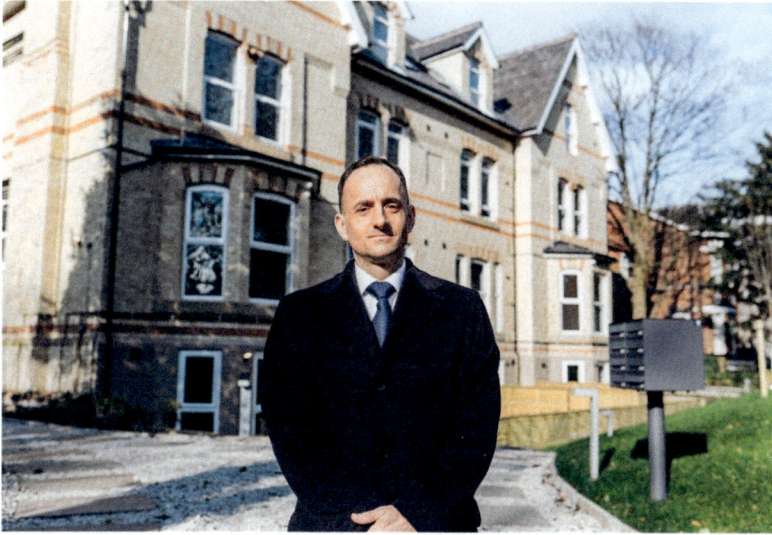

Peter Armistead is a graduate of Durham University and the College of Law, York. He spent six years as a lawyer in a top City law firm and then in an investment management company, before leaving the nine-to-five life to set up a property business and pursue his dream of skiing. In 50 months he purchased 50 properties, all whilst skiing over 200 days a year and running his business remotely from whichever part of the world he was travelling to.

He has successfully set up a property business which can be run from anywhere, enabling him to live wherever he chooses. Peter is an innovator, an investor, an award-winning developer and a business owner. He has bought and sold several hundred properties. He is a highly-accomplished skier and a competitive ultra mountain runner, having been on the podium for races at the 50k, 50 mile and 100 mile levels.

He has worked in over 30 different countries and currently lives in Whistler, BC where he works, skis and runs every day.

31074346R00088